Obama and China's Rise

OBAMA AND CHINA'S RISE

An Insider's Account of America's Asia Strategy

JEFFREY A. BADER

BROOKINGS INSTITUTION PRESS
Washington, D.C.

Copyright © 2012
THE BROOKINGS INSTITUTION
1775 Massachusetts Avenue, N.W., Washington, D.C. 20036
www.brookings.edu

Library of Congress Cataloging-in-Publication data
Bader, Jeffrey A.
  Obama and China's rise : an insider's account of America's Asia strategy / Jeffrey A. Bader.
      p.   cm.
  Summary: "Detailed evaluation from an insider of the Obama administration's efforts, between 2009 and spring 2011, to develop a stable relationship with China while countering China's rise by reinforcing and initiating relationships with other nations in the region"—Provided by the publisher.
  Includes bibliographical references and index.
  ISBN 978-0-8157-2242-7 (hardcover : alk. paper)
  1. United States—Foreign relations—China. 2. China—Foreign relations—United States. 3. Obama, Barack—Political and social views. 4. United States—Foreign relations—2009– 5. United States—Foreign relations—Asia. 6. Asia—Foreign relations—United States. I. Title.
  E183.8.C5B216 2012
  327.73051—dc23   2012000300

9 8 7 6 5 4 3 2 1

Printed on acid-free paper

Typeset in Adobe Caslon

Composition by R. Lynn Rivenbark
Macon, Georgia

Printed by R. R. Donnelley
Harrisonburg, Virginia

Contents

PREFACE

As an amateur historian in my younger days, I was amused, and slightly irritated, by Voltaire's epigram, "History is a pack of lies we play on the dead." The weighty, thoughtful, heavily footnoted history tomes I read, admired, and learned from as a graduate student seemed to deserve a more sympathetic characterization. Having now spent close to thirty years working on foreign policy for the U.S. government in various capacities, I have a greater appreciation of the insight of Voltaire's epigram, at least insofar as historians try to write about the actions of government officials of long ago. In this book I hope I can help future historians avoid the pitfalls that Voltaire warned about.

It is hard enough when you are inside an institution to understand how decisions are made. To do so at a distance of years is doubly hard. While distance in time and space may increase the ability to form dispassionate judgments, it also removes one from the richness of the context in which people argued over a proper course. It is tempting to attribute decisions with large consequences to large historical forces. Sometimes they are made in response to much narrower sets of concerns—personal, political, or bureaucratic.

The internal memoranda on which historians inevitably rely heavily may not reflect the realities behind decisions, particularly in the current atmosphere of perpetual anxiety over the risk of leaks and tendentious characterization of an administration's motives. It is often better to cloak a position in written high-mindedness than to acknowledge the quid pro quos or the political trade-offs involved.

In addition, all senior policymakers have drummed into them the risks of committing certain kinds of reasoning or calculations to paper. The e-mail saying "Let's discuss" is shorthand for "We're not going to correspond about this subject because what we might say in trying to reach a sensible decision could be held against us." This means that the written record will invariably be incomplete, and sometimes misleading. These habits of communication have run through every administration I have worked with since 1975. The only new element is the increasing likelihood of unwelcome and politically driven public scrutiny in the modern age of digital communication and ubiquitous media and blogs with a stake in pouncing on every supposed story, which has induced even greater caution within the government.

I hope in writing this book to simplify the task of future historians more gifted than I in understanding what went on in one important phase of Barack Obama's presidency, namely, his policy toward Asia at a time when China was rising. My account is based on my direct experiences and recollections, not on secondhand accounts or on documentary study. I have not had to see things through a filter, beyond the limits of my own experience and prejudices. My accounts of events may be incomplete because of these limitations, but I hope they will be a useful primary source for people trying to understand these events.

The book is essentially a memoir, a personal recounting of what I saw, what I did, and what I thought during the time I worked for President Obama. It may therefore occasionally appear as if I have attributed an outsized role to my own actions and slighted those who were more influential. I think that is an inevitable product of the memoir form, rather than an attempt by me to overstate my actions. Other accounts will flesh out the role of more senior players. It will then be for historians to sift through these accounts and make the necessary judgments about the accuracy and weighting of different versions.

I signed up to work for President Obama because of my profound admiration for the man whom I met in 2005 and whose extraordinary campaign for the presidency in 2007–08 unequivocally produced history. My time working for Barack Obama only increased my admiration and my conviction that he is an exceptional, once-a-century American political figure. A colleague told me that in twenty years she had never seen Obama lose his temper or raise his voice. I had only a little over two years' experience, but he certainly did not break that record in my time. I saw him in scores of meetings, and there was never an occasion in my mind in which he was not the most impressive figure in the room—the calmest, the most intellectually curious, the most eloquent, the most incisive, and the most authoritative. With foreign leaders, he moved seamlessly from his script to intense but respectful interchanges, invariably figuring out how to make the points that his staff had proposed, but in a way most likely to have an impact on the target audience rather than simply to register a point. He switched gears for the requisite three-minute statements to the media and without the benefit of notes delivered thoughtful accounts of what had just happened and what should happen next while his staff were left shaking their heads in admiration. He stoically suffered the indignities of modern American political character assassination without complaining or venting. Above all, in my experience he always wanted to do the right thing on foreign policy, not the politically expedient. Not only do I have no regrets over my time working for him; I will treasure it as the high point of my professional life.

I had superb colleagues to work with in the White House and National Security Council (NSC) who made the pressure cooker life there not only exhilarating but also enjoyable. My right-hand man was my senior deputy for Korea and Japan, Danny Russel. He was the single most effective and prolific foreign service officer I had ever met, born for the job at NSC and now my successor as senior director. My daily conversations with Danny guided my own thinking and helped us shape the Obama policy of strong relations with our Asian allies. My deputy for China, Evan Medeiros, is a rising star in the China field and will provide wisdom for decades as we adjust to the world featuring a rising China.

Tom Donilon was my boss as deputy and then national security adviser throughout my time at the White House. No one worked harder, with more dedication to the president and the national interest, than Tom. He is known around Washington as a political insider, but he is much more than that. He takes very seriously his responsibility to provide the best advice, and options, to the president without regard to domestic political impact, and he did that throughout our time together. He ran a highly effective Principals and Deputies Committee process that drove foreign policy and sacrificed his personal welfare to a degree beyond the usual to serve the president.

The deputy national security adviser during my last five months was Denis McDonough, who deserves special recognition. Having a close relationship with the president, Denis was frequently the transmission belt between staff and the Oval Office. Like Tom, he understood that his job was a sacred trust. He took advice well and made those of us who worked with him feel we were in a band of brothers.

On the economic team, Larry Summers and Mike Froman were an incomparable duo. A friend of mine once said of another towering American political figure, "America almost never produces quirky geniuses the way Europe does." Larry proved him wrong. Lots of people in Washington are bright. Not like Larry. It was mortifying to present Larry with an argument and then have him deconstruct it, drawing out the absurd and destructive implications of what you were saying in ways you never imagined when you made it. I always emerged from a conversation with Larry feeling my brain had been at least temporarily jolted out of neutral gear. Mike was the perfect foil for Larry—relentlessly practical and operational, a doer, the classic bureaucratic case of the person who ends up with every important task on a backbreaking schedule because he gets things done.

The other NSC senior directors and colleagues who sacrificed their personal lives enriched my life and work immeasurably. Standing out from the large group of exceptional public servants were Dennis Ross, Ben Rhodes, Samantha Power, Richard Reed, Mark Lippert, Gary Samore, Mike McFaul, and Puneet Talwar, with whom I worked on a slew of sensitive issues. Mike Hammer and Ben Chang in the Press Office did their best to smooth my rough edges in interacting with an unruly press corps and facilitated some accurate and insightful coverage of what we were doing.

Friends in other agencies provided exceptional guidance and support as well. At the State Department, Hillary Clinton was extraordinarily kind, gracious, warm, and inclusive, allowing me to function within her inner circle without the reserve that bureaucratic rivalry normally imposes on State-NSC interaction. Assistant Secretary of State Kurt Campbell was my daily thought and telephone partner as we worked to map out together an Asia policy serving America, the president, and the secretary. Kurt's creativity and deep knowledge of Asia made him a gifted policy formulator and spokesperson, with whom I agreed on policy 90 percent of the time and with whom I worked out the 10 percent where we did not. My mentor at State was Deputy Secretary Jim Steinberg, who was the administration's best foreign policy analyst and framer of issues as well as its deepest thinker on Asia. I had the privilege of traveling to Asia frequently as Jim's sidekick, and in doing so helping to shape thinking in Beijing, Seoul, and Tokyo. He is truly irreplaceable and will be sorely missed. Alan Romberg, Bob Suettinger, and Victor Cha made uniformly helpful suggestions on my draft. So did colleagues at the Brookings Institution's John L. Thornton China Center: Ken Lieberthal, Cheng Li, and Jonathan Pollack. My research assistants at Brookings, Robert O'Brien and Meara Androphy, provided invaluable support. Teresa Hsu and Iris An, also with the Thornton China Center, made important contributions to the book. The China-U.S. Exchange Foundation generously provided support. The Brookings Institution and its chairman, John Thornton, provided encouragement and support for me to undertake this project. Brookings president Strobe Talbott offered excellent suggestions and edits. The team at Brookings Institution Press did a wonderful job in clarifying my prose and putting together this volume.

My partner for life is my wife Rohini Talalla. To reduce her impact on my life to the professional sphere would be absurd, but it has been huge in that domain. Malaysian by birth and American by choice, Rohini possesses a personal understanding of Asia that I have struggled as an outsider to acquire. She has kept me both conceptually and morally grounded as I have wrestled with numerous policy issues over the two and a half decades we have known each other, especially in the two plus years I worked for President Obama. She has brought a network of friends, experts, luminaries, and officials from and knowledgeable about Asia into our lives, to our personal and professional benefit.

But Rohini is not merely an exceptional professional partner. She is my inspiration, my lodestar, and the love of my life. Without her, my life would be immeasurably poorer in every way. This book is written in tribute and gratitude to her.

PROLOGUE:
THE CANDIDATE AND THE CAMPAIGN

I MET BARACK Obama in June 2005 over a Thai takeout dinner in a small unprepossessing conference room in his Senate office. I had been asked to join a meeting with him to discuss an obscure issue, whether or not the Senate should approve the Central America Free Trade Agreement (CAFTA) negotiated by the George W. Bush administration. Obama was one of a handful of Democratic senators who had not yet taken a position on the agreement, and he wanted to discuss the pros and cons with a few Democrats with experience in trade issues.

It was not altogether clear why I had been invited, since I had no experience with Central America. I had served as assistant U.S. trade representative in 2001–02, and in that capacity I had completed the negotiations on the accession of China into the World Trade Organization, so I had some public identity on trade issues, but in an entirely different part of the world.

I had, of course, seen Senator Obama's extraordinary speech to the Democratic National Convention in 2004 that catapulted him to national prominence. I was impressed by his eloquence and vision, but I do not as a rule tender my affections to charismatic speech-making politicians. Speeches are performances, not revelations of character. The ability to deliver a great speech is a huge asset for a politician, particularly in our media-drenched age, but it tells very little about decisionmaking abilities, intellect, thoughtfulness, temperament, leadership, or management skills.

So I admired the man I had seen on the television that night, but I did not feel any sense of personal commitment to the one I was meeting that evening.

I was very curious, however. I am a moderate Democrat and was interested in seeing a fresh figure who had chosen not to fall into lockstep with the rest of his caucus on trade. As a former foreign service officer who had spent my entire adult life defending and formulating U.S. foreign policy, I was determined to see a Democratic nominee emerge who could win and turn around what I saw as the damaging and wrong-headed policies of the Bush years. I was skeptical of Hillary Clinton's candidacy, seeing her as a front runner based on her husband's name rather than demonstrated talents (indeed, I had a long-standing resistance to candidates whose rise derived from their family ties, including the post-JFK Kennedys, and my negative view of such candidates was heightened by the presidency of George W. Bush). My later exposure to Clinton as secretary of state fundamentally altered my view of her, but that experience was two years into the future.

I was not prepared for the man I encountered. I expected a small-room version of the charismatic orator from 2004—a voluble, outgoing, florid interlocutor. Within seconds, I knew I had vastly misread the man. He was calm, direct, thoughtful, and engaged. He locked eyes with each person in the room when introductions were exchanged. He spoke deliberately, choosing his words with care and precision. He projected considerable self-confidence, but not arrogance.

I felt transported back to a night in August 1960, when as a fifteen-year-old in New Hampshire's White Mountains I had listened to a squawking static-filled broadcast of the Democratic National Convention in Los Angeles, straining to hear whether John F. Kennedy would win the requisite number of votes on the first ballot and thereby avoid the danger of a brokered convention. I remembered the roar when at the end of the alphabet, Wyoming cast sufficient votes for Kennedy to put him over the top.

I do not have a track record of acute sensitivity to political rising stars. In this instance, however, I knew within minutes that the man across the table from me would run for president some day and would have an excellent chance of winning. He seemed to have the right combination of charisma and thoughtfulness, the ability to project vision and grandeur as well as to argue the fine points of an issue. He spoke of his sense of responsibility on the upcoming CAFTA vote, saying wryly, "I am the number ninety-nine senator in terms of seniority, but I seem to be getting wildly disproportionate attention, overwhelmingly for the wrong reasons." He noted that while he did not want to lightly break with his caucus, he fundamentally believed in the importance of trade and regarded many arguments on the left against trade agreements as disguised protectionism. He might in the end choose to vote against the agreement, he said, but he wanted to distinguish himself from others in his party, perhaps through a speech he planned to give a few days later in Illinois—both of which he ultimately did.[1]

Our discussion lasted three hours. It did not leave me with a clear sense of his views on foreign policy, which was not the principal subject of the evening. But it did convey a measure of the man, convincing me that if he ever ran for president, I wanted to be with him.

Twenty months later, on a cold day in Springfield, Illinois, Senator Obama announced his candidacy for president. Polls showed him capturing one-quarter as many votes as Senator Clinton. His candidacy was judged quixotic, perhaps preparing him for a brighter day in 2012 or beyond.

A few days later, I bumped into Susan Rice in the lobby of the Brookings Institution, where she and I worked. I knew Susan from our days in the Clinton administration when I was ambassador to Namibia and she was assistant secretary of state for African affairs. I had heard that she was a top foreign policy adviser to the Obama campaign. I told her I had met Obama, been profoundly impressed, and wanted to work on the campaign. She reacted positively, and shortly after she and Tony Lake, former national security adviser and head of the Obama campaign foreign policy team, asked me to cochair the senator's Asia advisory team with my friend Mona Sutphen (subsequently named deputy chief of staff in the Obama White House).

I had had considerable experience over the preceding three decades working on U.S. policy toward Asia, especially China. I had entered the Asia field in the State Department in 1977 when by serendipity I landed a job as staff assistant to Richard Holbrooke, then assistant secretary of state for East Asian affairs. Holbrooke, a force of nature even early in his dazzling diplomatic career, became my professional godfather. When the

United States established diplomatic relations with China during his tenure, I studied the Chinese language and entered the China field, where I spent most of my own career over the next two decades at the State Department, the National Security Council (NSC), and the Office of the U.S. Trade Representative. I had been involved in many of the key events in U.S.-China relations during that period, including the establishment of diplomatic relations, the passage of the Taiwan Relations Act, the building of close ties in the 1980s, the disputes over proliferation of weapons of mass destruction, the reaction to the Tiananmen massacre of 1989, the Taiwan Strait tensions of 1995–96, the exchange of state visits between President Jiang Zemin and President Bill Clinton in 1997–98, and China's accession to the World Trade Organization. I knew many of the key players in U.S. foreign policy in both parties who were engaged in Asia policy.

But I had no experience whatsoever in electoral or campaign politics. While a Democrat, my entire career had been one of sworn loyalty to the president of whichever party was in power, a role I filled comfortably and without chafing. I have always believed that foreign policy should be nonpartisan and bipartisan, so I was as proud to serve the Reagan administration as I was that of Clinton. I was ill prepared for the requirements of presidential campaigns, in which issues are important but finding large or small advantage over one's opponent is more so.[2]

Our Asia advisory team at the outset consisted of six lonely folks— Mona Sutphen, Michael Schiffer, D. L. McNeal, Derek Mitchell, Matt Goodman, and myself. Mona had served on the NSC staff in the second Clinton administration, and I had gotten to know her there. Michael, an expert on Northeast Asia, was a former foreign policy staffer to Senator Dianne Feinstein. D. L. was a colleague at the China Center at Brookings and supremely knowledgeable about the ins and outs of African American politics, among other subjects. Matt, like Mona, was a colleague of mine at Stonebridge International (a consulting group where I worked from 2002 to 2005), a former NSC official in the George W. Bush years, and an expert on Japan. Derek, also an expert on East Asia, was a scholar at the Center for Strategic and International Studies who had worked on China at the Defense Department in the Clinton administration. Mona and D. L. were the only ones in our group with natural domestic political instincts. But we complemented each other very well, got along, and had a grand time during the roller coaster ride of the next twenty months.

Outside advisers in a campaign, contrary to the assumption of some Washington pundits looking for clues about a candidate's thinking, are by and large expected to be seen as names on mastheads, not heard. We understood that the campaign was overwhelmingly about domestic issues, primarily economic, and that foreign policy was traditionally viewed as a weakness of Democratic candidates. All of us were by conviction internationalists who believed in American global leadership. We in no way resembled the caricature Republicans have painted of Democrats as naïve about international power realities since the McGovern candidacy of 1972. But we also were profoundly dismayed by the contempt in which the country was held by the rest of the world as the Bush era ground to a close, and we were determined to reverse it.

For the most part, this did not involve dramatic changes in U.S. policy toward East Asia. The Bush foreign policy team included a number of people—notably Colin Powell, Bob Zoellick, Rich Armitage, Jim Kelly, and Doug Paal—who well understood the requirements and subtleties of a sound Asia policy. They had to fight bruising internal battles with a shifting coalition of neoconservatives and hard-liners, but they achieved a number of positive outcomes in the Asian region. Korea policy was the subject of twists and turns and considerable infighting, and no one, including the chief advocates of the policy, was satisfied with the outcomes or the process.[3] Except for issues where the infighting produced distortions, such as with North Korea, the problems in U.S. leadership in Asia were not the consequence of Asia-specific policy errors, but rather of the spillover of misguided U.S. policies elsewhere in the world that had consequences everywhere.

So our campaign team did not see our role as that of articulating dramatic new policy initiatives to reverse eight years of Asia policy. Our objective was more to present a responsible Asia policy to a public skeptical of Democratic talent in that sphere, one embodying leadership, a greater presence in the area, strengthening of relationships with allies, a realistic approach toward China, openness toward multilateral institution building in the Asia-Pacific, and increased attention to Southeast Asia. Initiatives would follow, not precede, the election. In the meantime, we wanted to help our candidate position himself in the mainstream of U.S. foreign policy since World War II and not allow him to be depicted as a radical or as Jimmy Carter redux, that is, as a moralistic naïf unable or unwilling to defend American interests.

Mainly, we provided questions and answers for debate preparation, press guidance for daily reactions to stories in East Asia, background materials for Senator Obama on major issues, and an occasional article on Obama's foreign policy thinking, usually for publication in foreign journals. We understood that East Asian allies needed reassurance that Obama, with whom they were not familiar, was a friend, so we placed a good deal of emphasis on outreach to foreign political figures, foreign publications, and foreign scholars. We did not want to see a narrative develop in the region about the risks of an unproven candidate, with possible consequences both for the campaign and for future policy. We sent our materials daily to the campaign's chief foreign policy advisers Denis McDonough, Mark Lippert, Susan Rice, and Tony Lake (the former two had served on Obama's Senate staff, while the latter two, as noted earlier, had been senior officials in the Clinton administration).

As the spring of 2008 rolled around and Senator Obama established a clear lead over Senator Clinton, our band of six was approached by a growing number of people who had stood on the sidelines or been in the Clinton camp wishing to join our operation. We slowly expanded it, first to about twenty by May-June and ultimately to sixty for the campaign against Senator John McCain in the fall. Although some joined anticipating a payoff in an administration job, almost all evinced the enthusiasm and sense of mission for Senator Obama's historic candidacy that our original six felt.

For the most part, we tried to channel the group's enthusiasm in ways that did not distract from campaign priorities by making waves or committing gaffes. That meant, for example, not chasing after Senator McCain's foreign policy credentials with attempts to match article for article, to avoid the risk of shifting campaign attention to McCain's preferred issues. In one instance, that meant putting down a mini-rebellion among our Japan experts anxious to rebut three articles Senators McCain and Joseph Lieberman published in the Japanese media on Asia policy, instead relying on surrogates to defend the Obama position. In other cases, it meant muting the public expressions of ardor for the U.S.-Korea

Free Trade Agreement by members of the group, with whom it was universally popular, because of the difficulty of defending an unequivocal pro–free trade position in the Midwest. It also meant adjudicating differences on policy toward North Korea within our group, which mirrored the fierce debates of the last decade and a half on how to deal with the country's nuclear weapons program.

With Senator Obama's victory on November 4, our Asia group, like all the other foreign policy groups, disbanded. The transition team, whose foreign policy group was cochaired by Susan Rice, soon to be ambassador to the United Nations, and James Steinberg, soon to be deputy secretary of state, quickly formed a new, much more compact group in which I was designated the lead on the Asia-Pacific. A handful of others from the Asia-Pacific team in the campaign, notably Mona Sutphen, Michael Schiffer, Frank Jannuzi, and Matt Goodman, continued to work in the transition team.[4]

I had joined the Obama campaign in 2007 with no interest in returning to government. Sixty-three years old and making a decent living in the private sector after twenty-seven years of economic struggle as a foreign service officer, I did not wish to return to federal government pay scales as I prepared for retirement.

In December, however, Mark Lippert, who was emerging as a key link between the foreign policy team and the president-elect, asked me if I would be interested in serving as senior director for Asia at the National Security Council. I had previously served at the NSC in a more junior capacity and regarded it as a superb place to work, all the more so in an Obama administration of historic import. Mark subsequently arranged for me to meet General Jim Jones, the national security adviser designate, who assured me that as senior director for Asia I would have direct and frequent access to the president. I was skeptical, having seen how previous NSC teams worked and the limitations on senior directors' direct access to the president, but I felt this was an opportunity I could not afford to pass up. So I said yes.

ONE

ASIA POLICY:
THE BIG PICTURE

UNDER THE GEORGE W. Bush administration, U.S. policies toward most of the major countries in Asia were generally sound. President Bush arbitrated between his administration's warring factions—broadly speaking, pragmatic moderates and neoconservatives—that plagued his foreign policy elsewhere and put in place a policy toward China that maintained stability through most of his two terms. His warm relationship with Prime Minister Junichiro Koizumi of Japan facilitated cooperation on international issues, while the administration did important work to strengthen the U.S.-Japan alliance, developing military coordination and realigning U.S. bases in Japan. The U.S.-India relationship also moved forward with an agreement on peaceful uses of nuclear energy. On the other hand, the attempt to pursue a coherent Korea policy proved difficult. Battles between the Office of the Vice President and the State Department produced two competing policy lines, with further strains being created by a leader in Seoul who seemed less than fully committed to the alliance. Meanwhile, Southeast Asia was substantially neglected.

Thus from its earliest days the Obama team felt the next administration would be inheriting a mixed bag in the Asia department—some achievements and some deficiencies. But it also understood that governing would be different from campaigning. Though we tried to lay out some broad directions in which we planned to take Asia policy, we knew that actual decisions would need to be informed by an interagency process providing a deeper grasp of the issues than could be acquired during a campaign.

It seemed clear, however, that whatever successes the Bush administration had achieved in the region, they were contaminated by the fallout from problems elsewhere. As our team quickly learned, the general perception in Asia in 2009 was that the United States was distracted by the war in Iraq and global war on terrorism and was economically weakened.

In her four-year tenure, Secretary of State Condoleezza Rice had missed two of the annual meetings of the Association of Southeast Asian Nations Regional Forum (ARF).[1] Like a number of other Asian multilateral forums, the ARF is not a place of collective decisionmaking or consequential actions, so the long trek to Asia for the event is considered a tedious task by many U.S. officials, particularly secretaries of state invariably preoccupied with urgent crises elsewhere. But Asian countries see such absences as confirmation that the United States does not give high priority to Asia: if the distance is too great to justify a visit for a conference, it must be too great for more serious commitments as well.

Asian commentators complained to our team that even when President Bush and the secretary of state attended major conferences or met with Asian leaders, they seemed to care mainly about terrorism and little about the economic issues worrying Asians. Indeed, the Bush administration attempted to change the agenda and focus of the Asia-Pacific Economic Cooperation (APEC) forum, which is explicitly dedicated to economic growth and coordination, to include substantial discussion of terrorism.[2]

Further problems were simmering in Southeast Asia's largest Muslim-majority countries, Indonesia and Malaysia. The global war on terrorism had profoundly damaged America's image throughout the Islamic world, bringing favorable attitudes down to the single and low double digits in Indonesian polls. Similarly disaffected, Malaysia continued to pursue anti-American "nonaligned" policies inherited from former prime minister Mahathir Mohamad. With hostility running high in such countries, it was difficult for them to align with the United States on most issues, including vital ones such as Iran, Iraq, Afghanistan, and economic problems.[3]

The major geostrategic challenge facing Asia, and the United States in Asia, was how to react to the dramatic rise of China in the previous decade. China's spectacular economic growth, averaging 10 percent a year, and its thorough integration into the economies of the region through a web of trade and investment had permanently altered the geopolitical landscape. At the end of the Bush administration, China owned about $1 trillion in U.S. government-guaranteed debt, which amounted to about a tenfold leap since 2001. The trade deficit with China was about $250 billion annually, by far America's largest bilateral deficit. These developments had left many Americans feeling vulnerable to the apparent leverage from Chinese ownership of U.S. debt as well as angry at what they considered unfair trading practices producing the sizable deficit. Countries of the region were in addition anxious about China's military spending, which had grown at an even faster pace than its economy.

Containment in the style of U.S. policy toward the Soviet Union after World War II was not a plausible option. China was now completely integrated into the global economy and indeed had been explicitly encouraged by the United States to move in this direction since the Nixon administration. The assumption was that China could thus play a more constructive role than it would by sitting outside of that system, a theory that had been borne out in practice. Nor did China appear to harbor the global imperial aspirations of the former Soviet Union.[4] Nevertheless, uncertainties and anxieties shrouded China's emergence.[5]

It was clear to the Obama team that a unidimensional approach to China would yield unsatisfactory results. U.S policy toward a rising China could not rely solely on military muscle, economic blandishments, and pressure and sanctions on human rights, an overall strategy that had not been notably successful in altering unwelcome Chinese actions even when China was weaker. At the same time, a policy of indulgence and accommodation of assertive Chinese conduct, or indifference to its internal evolution, could embolden bad behavior and frighten U.S. allies and partners. We would spend a good deal of effort during my time at the National Security Council fine-tuning an approach that avoided these extremes and ensured that the U.S. presence in Asia would be strengthened to allay the concerns of other countries in the face of a rising China.

Our team also concluded that more active U.S. participation in regional organizations was a necessary component of an effective Asia policy. Asia was an alphabet soup of such groups, each composed largely of top-level members of state. These included the Association of Southeast Asian Nations (ASEAN), the Asia-Pacific Economic Cooperation forum

(APEC), the East Asia Summit (EAS), the ASEAN Plus Three (ASEAN, China, Japan, and South Korea), the ASEAN Regional Forum, and the Shanghai Cooperation Organization (an organization consisting of Russia, China, and four central Asian states formerly part of the Soviet Union). In addition, there were regular trilateral meetings among high-level authorities of the most important countries, for example, China, Russia, and India or China, South Korea, and Japan.

For the most part, the Bush administration had stood aside from the development of regional organizations and meetings, in particular declining to seek participation in the newly created annual East Asia Summit. It did so for several reasons: it was somewhat skeptical about the effectiveness of multilateral institutions, believed that unfocused organizations were little more than talk shops, and felt uncertain about which organization would emerge as most important.[6] By contrast, our team believed that an America embedded in emerging multilateral institutions would give comfort to countries uncertain about the impact of China's rise and provide important balance and leadership, a view influenced by that of regional leaders like Australia's prime minister Kevin Rudd, Indonesia's president Susilo Bambang Yudhoyono, and Singapore's prime minister Lee Hsien Loong.

Beyond hoping to demonstrate greater emphasis on Asia than under the previous administration, Obama faced challenges inherent in some Asian suspicions about the policies of the Democratic Party and of past Democratic administrations in dealings with Asia. Especially, but not exclusively, many in Japan, have long held that Republicans care more about U.S. alliances and are more reliable supporters of forward-deployed defense. Japanese pundits frequently argue that Democrats are pro-China, whereas Republicans are pro-Japan (a notion that persists despite the undeniable fact that the greatest shock to U.S.-Japan relations since 1960 occurred during a Republican administration, when President Richard M. Nixon tilted toward China). Memories of President Jimmy Carter's rash decision in 1977, subsequently reversed, to withdraw U.S. troops from South Korea continued to nurture suspicions in that regard.[7]

More broadly, many throughout the dynamic countries of East Asia felt a deep concern that the Democratic Party was protectionist and would erect barriers to free trade that would negatively affect their economies. There was a credible basis for this concern. President Bill Clinton's attempt to renew "fast-track" authority that would allow him to negotiate trade agreements without debilitating congressional amendments had attracted only forty votes within the House Democratic caucus, much to the president's chagrin. Furthermore, the Democratic Party's long and close ties with labor unions wary of the disruptions caused by trade have an impact on the voting behavior of congressional Democrats. Indeed, during the campaign, both candidates Obama and Hillary Clinton came out against the U.S.-South Korea Free Trade Agreement negotiated by the Bush administration, despite the palpable economic benefits the United States would garner if it went into effect. Rhetoric about the negative effect of imports from China and Chinese trade practices also featured in the campaign, primarily from the Clinton side.

Traditional Democratic policies and rhetoric on human rights touched another nerve in Asia's democracies and autocracies alike. In their eyes, U.S. missionary zeal to promote democracy and human rights showed little regard for economic development, domestic stability, cultural sensitivities, and regional balance. Most Asian politicians and intellectuals favor the so-called Asian model of development, which led many of their countries to evolve in stages from poverty and one-party autocracies into prosperous middle-class societies with more liberal governments. For them, U.S. policy reflected a cookie-cutter approach, with its talk of universal values and attempt to treat every country the same regardless of key differences in their development. The exclusive association of this kind of human rights policy with the Democratic Party had been undercut by the Bush administration's "freedom agenda" and neoconservative calls for spreading democracy. But the "freedom agenda" was widely viewed as pure rhetoric with no real implementation in Asia, so was easily dismissed. Asians were not so sure what to expect from President Obama, whose entire biography was a triumph of human rights, and from Secretary Clinton, whose advocacy for the rights of women, the poor, and the disadvantaged had featured so prominently in her career and notably in her appearance at the Beijing United Nations Women's Conference in 1995.

Like candidate Obama, our foreign policy team dealing with Asia was resolutely pragmatic and nonideological. We did not have the splits of the Bush team, of course, between neoconservatives and traditional realists. But we also did not have distinct center and left camps divided along traditional fault lines such as trade, human rights and democracy promotion, or military deployment and spending. Naturally our people placed different weights on issues, but they did not fall into camps or factions. The team's core beliefs centered on alliances with America's democratic partners, a sustained forward deployment in Asia, a relationship with China that would enable us to expand areas of cooperation and manage differences, free flows of trade and investment, and giving Asia higher overall priority in our foreign policy.

The president and his spokespersons were not focused on the balance of power or Realpolitik. As Henry Kissinger's magisterial *Diplomacy* makes clear, for the past century American leaders of both parties have echoed the democracy promotion agenda and norm-based internationalism of Woodrow Wilson.[8] Likewise, the Obama administration has emphasized developing and strengthening adherence to international norms. But underlying our approach was a clear understanding that our political, security, and economic policies in Asia needed to be grounded in traditional state-to-state relations and a commitment to shaping the choices of emerging powers like China through our diplomacy and deployments. That meant our policies toward the region's actors—allies like Japan, Korea, and Australia, as well as emerging players and partners like China, India, Indonesia, and Vietnam—needed to reflect these linkages and avoid developing tunnel vision. Obama therefore believed that such countries should be given a larger role in economic institutions like the Group of 20 (G-20), which included Japan, Korea, Australia, China, India, and Indonesia, and he was predisposed to consider joining multilateral institutions that would recognize the important role of these countries.

This landscape led the Obama foreign policy team to several fundamental strategic judgments about the Asia-Pacific region, the actors in it, and American interests there. We treated these judgments not as a catechism in our daily decisionmaking, but more as an essential framework for our decisions and actions. Some strategic principles were relatively clear to the foreign policy team at the outset. Others would become more evident as events requiring responses unfolded. Their key elements can be summarized as follows:

—The Asia-Pacific region deserved higher priority in American foreign policy. With wealth, power, and influence gradually shifting from

Europe toward Asia in the past several decades, the region has emerged as the world's center of gravity for economic, political, and security decisions in the twenty-first century.

—The major strategic development in the region and arguably the whole world is the emergence of China as a major power that by most measures appears poised to become the second most influential country on the globe within a generation.

—America's relationship with China could be shaped to maximize the chances that China's rise will become a stabilizing and constructive force rather than a threat to peace and equilibrium.

—A sound China strategy should rest on three pillars: (1) a welcoming approach to China's emergence, influence, and legitimate expanded role; (2) a resolve to see that its rise is consistent with international norms and law; and (3) an endeavor to shape the Asia-Pacific environment to ensure that China's rise is stabilizing rather than disruptive.

—America's key alliances with Japan, South Korea, and Australia are critical to maintaining a framework of peace and stability in the region, as is developing effective political and security partnerships with other emerging and important actors, including Indonesia, India, and Vietnam.

—A U.S. foreign policy based on a weak domestic economy will ultimately be a failure. Rebuilding leadership abroad depends on rebuilding economic strength at home.

—North Korea's emergence as a nuclear weapons state with ballistic missile capability is a threat to U.S. security. Past attempts to persuade North Korea to roll back its programs have failed or had limited success. We needed a policy that would force North Korea to reassess the value of its program and thereby maximize the chance of its pursuing denuclearization seriously. This required breaking the cycle of North Korean provocation, extortion, and accommodation (by China, Japan, Russia, South Korea, and the United States), and reward.

—A sustained and strong U.S. presence—economic, political, and security—is welcomed by most of the states of the region. They see the United States as a source of innovation, trade and investment, ideas, and educational opportunity; as the protector and provider of global public goods such as freedom of the seas and an open trade and investment system; as protector of the weak and defenseless against aggression; and as the necessary partner in responding to disasters. In their eyes, America is an essential stabilizing force as rising powers, principally China but also India, gain in influence.

—The United States must both participate and lead in the most important multilateral organizations in the region, including new ones with potential political and security roles. A stronger U.S. relationship with Southeast Asia, and ASEAN, is both an end in itself and an underpinning of a broader Asian equilibrium.

—The advancement of human rights requires a multipronged approach that treats different situations differently. In some instances, this will call for greater engagement with foreign governments, civil society, and their military. Public clarity about abuses and shortcomings will be essential in all cases. Principles and values pertaining to human rights and democracy should be articulated so as to persuade, not to score points. The U.S. government should be clear, but respectful, and speak in a language and to issues that matter in the lives of the people of Asia.

TWO

LAYING THE FOUNDATION: SECRETARY CLINTON VISITS ASIA

DURING ITS TRANSITION and opening days, the Obama administration looked for ways to demonstrate that from the beginning it intended to place much greater emphasis on U.S. relations with Asia. Deputy National Security Adviser Tom Donilon argued that the United States needed to rebuild its presence and relations in parts of the world where it appeared distracted, which first of all meant East Asia.

Donilon and Denis McDonough, chief of staff of the National Security Council (NSC), called for early steps to demonstrate this new approach. Although the State Department's assistant secretary of state designate for East Asian and Pacific affairs, Kurt Campbell, was not confirmed by the Senate until June, he strongly supported an early trip to Asia by Secretary Hillary Clinton to demonstrate Asia's centrality to U.S. interests. Encouraged by her incoming deputy secretary of state James Steinberg, who had a long history of intensive involvement in Asian issues, Secretary Clinton decided to make her first overseas trip to Asia, the first time a secretary of state had done so since Asia-hand Dean Rusk visited it in 1961. The trip, to take place in February, was carefully structured to start with America's strongest ally in Asia, Japan; to include its other key ally, South Korea; to feature a stop in China to meet the leadership; and also to include Indonesia.

For a country with 250,000,000 people and the growing potential to be a regional leader, Indonesia had not gotten much attention from Washington. Our team wanted to fundamentally change the relationship with

Indonesia. We had multiple reasons, and multiple tools. The relationship had sunk to new depths after 9/11 and the Iraq war, clouded by the widespread view in Indonesia that the United States was anti-Islam. Favorable ratings of the United States were at historic lows. We believed that by pursuing a different policy in Iraq and reaching out in a new spirit to the Islamic world, President Obama, who had spent formative years in Indonesia and had Indonesian relatives, could dramatically change America's image and effectiveness there.

I traveled with Secretary Clinton on this first trip, on February 15–22, 2009, along with Assistant Secretary for East Asia and Pacific Chris Hill and Clinton's closest political aides and speechwriters. In advance of the trip, the secretary, her aides, and the NSC staff thought about what messages we wanted to convey at each stop, this being the first encounter these leaders would have with an authoritative figure in the new administration. Here is how we conceived the trip:

—*Japan*. Demonstrate the centrality of the alliance for the regional interests of both countries. Commit to more intensive consultations on the Six-Party Talks regarding North Korean nuclear disarmament.[1] Sign an agreement on Japanese assistance in moving the controversial U.S. Marine Corps Air Station from the busy town of Futenma to a smaller location in Okinawa.

—*Indonesia*. Demonstrate that we considered Indonesia a rising regional power and a global actor. Show support for the Association of Southeast Asian Nations (ASEAN), in which Indonesia is the dominant actor. Establish a comprehensive partnership with Indonesia covering economics, security, energy, and education.

—*South Korea*. Show that the United States stood shoulder-to-shoulder with Seoul in its stance on North Korea and could be counted on to defend South Korea. Cement ties with the South's president Lee Myung-bak. Consult with his government about the best way to pursue negotiations with the North on denuclearization. Discuss the free trade agreement with Seoul in a way that would keep it alive but not raise unrealistic hopes of an early agreement on steps leading to ratification.

—*China*. The Obama team had taken pains in the campaign to avoid the mistakes of the presidential campaigns of 1980, 1992, and 2000, which had damaged U.S.-China relations early on and taken anywhere from one to three years to get past. We wanted to put a floor under the relationship, to convey that we intended to expand areas of cooperation while managing differences. We believed that the Obama administration's highest priorities—denuclearization of Iran and North Korea, restoring the world economy, combating climate change, fighting terrorism in Afghanistan and Pakistan, ending the civil war and genocide in Sudan, and achieving energy security—all required, or at least would benefit from, Chinese cooperation. Our goal was to establish a relationship with a modicum of trust between U.S. and Chinese leaders so that there could be political incentives for cooperation.

The trip achieved what we set out to do. Secretary Clinton proved a tireless worker, scheduling days with up to sixteen events and meetings and performing superbly throughout. Displaying international rock star qualities, she elicited shrieks of approval from Asians and Americans gathered along her motorcade route, in hotel lobbies, or during her speeches. When she spoke at South Korea's main university for women, close to 2,000 star-struck girls with tears streaming down their faces were visibly moved, inspired by the ultimate woman's role model and avidly absorbing her every word.[2]

In Japan, Secretary Clinton met with relatives of people abducted by the North Korean security services between 1977 and 1983, a humanitarian gesture she felt important to prevent this issue from becoming politicized in U.S.-Japan relations, as it had been during the Bush administration. Her meeting with Foreign Minister Hirofumi Nakasone proceeded uneventfully and satisfactorily. As soon as the meeting with Prime Minister Taro Aso opened, the prime minister surprised us by suggesting that he could mediate for us with Iran since Japan had special connections there. We responded warily to an idea that did not seem fully thought through. In her meeting with the defense minister, Secretary Clinton properly departed from script by not agreeing to schedule a so-called two-plus-two meeting (with defense and foreign affairs ministers in one session), because the status of some alliance issues appeared uncertain and it was not even clear who would be in power when the meeting was held.[3]

Her biggest challenge in Japan proved to be how to deal with the head of the opposition Democratic Party of Japan (DPJ), Ichiro Ozawa. A legendary fixer and a godfather of Japanese money politics, Ozawa was preparing the DPJ for an upcoming election—in which it beat the Liberal Democratic Party (LDP), ending a fifty-four-year LDP monopoly on power except for a brief interlude in 1993–94. The U.S. embassy had been trying for weeks to set up a meeting for Clinton with Ozawa, but his office hedged on the scheduling, and only at the last minute did a 9 p.m. slot arise. Earlier that day, Ozawa gave an interview in which he called for a drastically reduced U.S. military presence in Japan and withdrawal of all forces except for the Seventh Fleet.[4] The question then was how Secretary Clinton should handle the meeting—whether to cancel, whether to say no pictures or press, what tone to take. She was less exercised than some of the rest of us, seeing Ozawa's behavior as that of a politician of a sort she recognized and declining to give him the gift of a snub. So the meeting proceeded, with Clinton remaining cool and correct and Ozawa somewhat defensive and almost apologetic. We came out of the meeting believing we could work with Ozawa, but it would be considerably more challenging than with the LDP.

The South Korea stop, while brief, got our relationship there off on the right foot. Secretary Clinton had a warm, unscripted meeting with Foreign Minister Yu Myung-hwan in which they saw eye-to-eye on how to deal with North Korea. Then over a small lunch, President Lee Myung-bak laid out eloquently and in some detail his views about the situation inside North Korea and ways we could approach Pyongyang. Lee found North Korea less monolithic now as news from the outside world seeped in, and he foresaw possibilities to affect its policies if the international community, especially South Korea and the United States, showed firmness and did not repeat previous acceptance of North Korean extortion. It was a stimulating roundtable discussion, without talking points, and Lee impressed all of us as a serious partner. He did not push the U.S.-South Korea Free Trade Agreement, demonstrating that he understood the dynamics of U.S. politics at that early point in the administration.[5]

Our principal goal was to make clear to the South Koreans that they could trust the Obama administration on the North Korean nuclear issue, that there would be no surprises. For reasons on both sides, the South's relationship with the previous administration had been troubled. The Bush administration had an internal war over how to respond to North Korea's nuclear weapons program. A group around Vice President Dick Cheney seemed to regard all negotiations as appeasement and favored actively seeking regime change, though the tools to do so were not evident. This view was shared by others, primarily in nonproliferation offices at the White House and State Department. On the other side, primarily in Bush's second term, Chris Hill led an aggressive effort to negotiate some kind of step-by-step process that could build momentum toward denuclearization. Hill was supported by Secretary of State Condoleezza Rice, and ultimately by President Bush, but the bureaucratic rivalries were so fierce that just getting negotiating instructions was torturous. Paralleling the confusion on the U.S. side, the South Korean government under President Roh Moo-hyun seemed desperate to reach any kind of deal with the North Koreans but was unable to use its leverage in any effective way. The result was a six-party approach that relied substantially on the diplomatic activism of Chris Hill, but with sullen resentment from the Japanese, limited buy-in by the South Koreans, and heavy reliance on the Chinese.[6]

By the time of Secretary Clinton's visit, our team had not developed details of a negotiating strategy. At this point, our goal was to firm up our relationships with the key players—first the South Koreans, then the Japanese, and finally the Chinese. We did not intend to roll out an uncoordinated new plan that would have dismayed our counterparts and had no chance of implementation.

We prepared for the Indonesia stop by holding several interagency meetings in Washington beforehand so when we arrived we had already made some consequential decisions. Many of us believed it was time for the United States to accede to the ASEAN Treaty of Amity and Cooperation (TAC). Negotiated in the 1980s, it is a feel-good agreement with no binding obligations on association members, essentially calling for a peaceful resolution of disputes—arguably of little consequence, but harmless. The ASEAN countries had long tried to cajole previous administrations into joining other non-ASEAN signatories, Russia, China, Australia, India, Japan, and France, as a member, but the U.S. had showed little interest for reasons as negligible as the treaty itself. Some believed accession would tie America's hands in Burma because U.S. sanctions might be labeled treaty violations. Some in the Defense Department felt the treaty's emphasis on noninterference in countries' internal affairs could negatively affect U.S. alliance commitments. With North Korea's accession to the TAC in 2008, some also argued that it could also affect America's North Korea policy. I felt these arguments were legally and substantively dubious. I worked with others to try to build a consensus to change the policy.

Happily, on the eve of the February 15 trip, Secretary Clinton hosted a dinner to which she invited outside Asia experts. I was slightly apprehensive because it was my first encounter with her since the primary campaign. She completely won me over that night with her extraordinary personal warmth and graciousness, something I did not expect given my recent history as an active backer of candidate Obama and an outspoken opponent of her candidacy. It made me see her in a way that blind identification and loyalties inherent in a political campaign had veiled earlier.

The dinner guests included former ambassador to Indonesia (and China) J. Stapleton Roy, one of American foreign policy's few remaining "wise men." Roy suggested to Secretary Clinton that we accede to TAC. She asked me what I thought. I said I agreed and indeed had been quietly working with other lower-ranking officials toward that end. She blessed the idea. At a Deputies Committee meeting chaired by Tom Donilon a few days later, and with Secretary Clinton's support, we blasted through concurrence over muted opposition from human rights advocates worried about the putative impact on Burma or North Korea policy. The State Department and the navy quickly produced written analyses explaining how to accede without detriment to U.S. interests (by essentially following the Australian example of saying that nothing in the agreement would affect U.S. policies and freedom of action), and Clinton carried that news to Jakarta. It was a remarkable turnaround on a long-standing, little-reviewed policy in a very short time span.

The administration's longer-term goal in signing the TAC was not so much to join one more seemingly insignificant convention but rather to lay the basis for possible accession to the East Asia Summit (EAS), potentially the most important regional organization in view of its ability to deal with political and security issues. It included all the key regional players—China, Japan, South Korea, India, Australia, New Zealand, and ASEAN—but not the United States. The Obama administration had not yet decided whether it wished to join, but we wanted to have that option. EAS membership required adherence to the TAC.

During the February trip, Secretary Clinton also became the first secretary of state to visit the headquarters of ASEAN, thereby making a symbolic gesture of support for the organization. She announced that the United States would appoint its first-ever Jakarta-based ambassador to

ASEAN, which it did in 2011. Both of these initiatives reflected Kurt Campbell's desire to increase America's footprint in Southeast Asia.

As usual, the stop in China received the greatest scrutiny. The Chinese government viewed the secretary with some wariness for two reasons. During the Beijing Women's Conference in 1995, she had delivered a speech strongly criticizing the heavy-handed way the Chinese ran the conference and treated the attending nongovernmental organizations (NGOs), thereby becoming a rallying-point for women and human rights critics. She also had issued some fairly hot rhetoric about China during the campaign, mostly on trade issues. While the Chinese leaders had a very good relationship with Bill Clinton, they were not sure if his spouse viewed China in the same light as he did.

Having spoken to Secretary Clinton a number of times about China, I was convinced that Chinese anxieties were overdrawn. She would be vocal on human rights, and she would be tough on trade issues, but these positions did not reflect an underlying hostility. I spoke privately to senior Chinese officials on the eve of the meetings to try to bring them to more realistic expectations and allay their apparent concerns.

Indeed, Secretary Clinton's presentations and interaction with the Chinese leaders were solid throughout her meetings with President Hu Jintao, State Councilor Dai Bingguo, and Foreign Minister Yang Jiechi. She consistently struck a tone of realism and cooperation, and our Chinese counterparts came away believing in her sincerity (so they told me). Although no breakthroughs occurred, there were no issues on which such developments could have been expected so early in the administration.[7]

As is often the case, the trip's major news story had nothing to do with what happened in any meeting but was the result of an offhand comment Secretary Clinton made to the press at the back of the plane on the way to Beijing. Responding to a question about human rights, she said that Americans always presented their points on human rights while the Chinese presented their points on Taiwan, and this was all predictable and resulted in formalistic exchanges. But this did not prevent the two from having serious exchanges on global issues such as security, the international economy, and climate change, where they needed to work together to make progress.[8]

Editorials and NGO comments purported to detect either a Clinton or Obama doctrine in these short remarks, suggesting they signified that

Secretary Clinton and the Obama administration were indifferent to human rights and were prepared to sacrifice human rights progress for global cooperation. These distorted interpretations became the hook for scores of opinion or news pieces attacking this supposed hallmark of administration policy. Some of these reactions were obviously sincere, but some also reflected an element of self-serving sensationalism, not only among the media but also among human rights NGOs that had a vested interest in calling attention to (and raising funds for) their worthy issues.[9]

Clinton's remarks were the classic Washington gaffe, namely, uttering an uncomfortable and politically incorrect truth publicly. Those who have been involved in U.S.-China relations know her characterization of the exchanges on human rights and Taiwan was exactly right. It is not that people haven't tried. I have seen some leaders highly committed to human rights, such as Bill Clinton, try to have a serious conversation with the Chinese on the subject, as he did with Jiang Zemin in 1997 and as I have. But the truth, recognized by every secretary of state since Henry Kissinger, is that our discussions of such issues have long tended overwhelmingly to be formulaic and without consequence. Secretary Clinton made the mistake of admitting it.

I suggested to Secretary Clinton the next morning that her formulation, while the absolute truth, was unduly provocative. I handed her a small yellow sheet with a few scribbled points, the essence of which was that protection of human rights was a critical global priority for the administration, and that we raise human rights concerns publicly and privately on all trips, as she had on this one. She accepted my comments and the paper without response, looking as if she were swallowing some bad-tasting medicine. In response to a question from Mark Landler of the *New York Times* at the press conference that day, she pulled out the paper I had given her and read the points in a deadpan without elaboration. The media and the NGOs were considerably less interested in this answer and continued to cite her earlier offhand comment as authoritative public policy. This served as an interesting reminder of the challenges of articulating foreign policy to the American public when some in the media were intent on stirring things up, even if the resulting characterizations had little or nothing to do with actual policy. The characterizations took on a life of their own and became easy targets for lazy analysts and useful themes for NGOs seeking to draw attention to their causes.

When Secretary Clinton organized a truly creative human rights event in Beijing, which was covered by Chinese media and bloggers, it received none of the public attention that her back-of-the-plane comment elicited. She invited sixteen prominent women involved in women's issues to a public forum at which many of them made very strong and courageous statements about the problems encountered in China and the failings of authorities—on HIV/AIDS and other health issues, professional discrimination, and sexual harassment and violence. Their comments were every bit as bold as what one might expect to hear at a U.S. town hall meeting. In my view, these kinds of events are worth more than a hundred sterile exchanges of talking points and breast-beating press releases.[10]

Our team wanted to take another early and highly visible symbolic step to demonstrate Asia's higher place in U.S. foreign policy priorities. We decided that the first foreign head of government to visit the Oval Office would be Japan's Prime Minister Aso, rather than the expected European dignitary (the United Kingdom's Gordon Brown seemed eager to be the first). This was not because of any particular affection for Aso, who, although a strong supporter of the U.S.-Japan alliance, carried some heavy baggage. His nationalism, combined with indiscretion and a propensity for politically incorrect and racially charged outbursts, made him a symbol of an earlier expansionist Japan, not only in China but also elsewhere in Asia. We all assumed Aso would not last long, but we judged it important to signal our commitment to the alliance by meeting with him first.

THREE

CHINA:
GETTING STARTED

WITH A NUMBER of negative examples from previous presidencies fresh in our minds, our team made China policy an early priority. For almost three decades, presidential transitions had damaged America's foreign policy interests, and we were determined to learn from that history.

THE UNHAPPY HISTORY
OF PRESIDENTIAL TRANSITIONS

In 1980, less than two years after President Jimmy Carter normalized relations with the People's Republic of China, Ronald Reagan took office having condemned Carter for abandoning America's ally, the Republic of China (Taiwan). Reagan indicated he intended to restore an official relationship with Taiwan and to sell it advanced fighter aircraft. Reagan's position was part of the Republican right's broader attack on the Carter administration but also on the legacy of Richard Nixon and Henry Kissinger, who had engineered the breakthrough to China and who represented in the group's minds an insufficiently principled policy of accommodating communists, whether in Moscow or in Beijing.[1]

The realities of governing, and of the cold war, quickly overtook Reagan's campaign promises, but not before the relationship with the People's Republic teetered on the brink of collapse, with the Soviet Union as the major potential beneficiary. Led by Secretary of State Alexander Haig, the Reagan administration backed down on its intention to sell advanced fighter jets to Taiwan and quickly engaged in a negotiation with Beijing on future arms sales to Taiwan. The outcome was a joint communiqué concluded on August 17, 1982, in which the United States pledged that its arms sales to Taiwan would not exceed in quality or quantity "the level of those supplied in recent years" and that it would phase out such sales to Taiwan over time, leading to "final resolution." The 1982 communiqué was not a crowning moment in the history of U.S. diplomacy, committing the United States to a diminution of arms sales to Taiwan that it could not carry out as Taiwan would have been left vulnerable to attack or pressure from the mainland. The U.S. implementation of the communiqué has, to understate the matter, been far from impressive, even before George H. W. Bush decided to sell F-16s to Taiwan during the 1992 presidential campaign. This has been the source of continuous friction with China since 1982 and has fed the Chinese belief that the United States has been acting in bad faith. The problem was not with the implementation (China's performance also did not live up to its promises), but with the communiqué's original conception, which stemmed directly from the Reagan campaign and administration's need to overcompensate for his intemperate critique of U.S.-China normalization.[2]

The next presidential transition occurred in 1989, a year that severely damaged U.S.-China relations, but through no fault of the incoming president, George H. W. Bush. It was the Tiananmen massacre of June 4 that kept relations deeply troubled for the remainder of the Bush presidency. U.S. sanctions were put in place, China's most favored nation (MFN)—that is, normal—trading status came under attack, and international cooperation became severely limited.

In 1992 candidate Bill Clinton famously denounced the "butchers of Beijing" for the 1989 massacre and the Bush administration's accommodation, and laid the groundwork for a policy requiring that Beijing fulfill human rights conditions before MFN status could be renewed. As a result, the relationship remained in the freezer for another couple of years, with sharp opposition to U.S. policy from all the states in the Asia-Pacific region as well as the U.S. business community. Just as a delayed and fragile renormalization was beginning to take place, the Taiwan Strait tensions of 1995–96 caused a further setback. Like the Reagan administration in 1982, the Clinton administration had to back down from its original punitive approach to China, walking away from the president's Executive Order 12850 of 1994 on conditional MFN, then painfully working its way back to a normal relationship through an exchange of state visits by the presidents of the two countries in 1997–98.

In 2000 candidate George W. Bush criticized the Clinton administration for supposedly considering China a "strategic partner," labeling it a "strategic competitor" instead.[3] Upon assuming office, the Bush administration was staffed by senior officials who were sharply divided on how to deal with China. On one side were traditional engagers, led by Secretary of State Colin Powell and U.S. Trade Representative Robert Zoellick, who sought continuity in relations with China. On the other side were a group concentrated in the Office of the Vice President and the senior leadership of the Defense Department, who sought to give policy toward China a new and harder edge. The split came out into the open in April 2001 after a Chinese pilot died in a collision between a U.S. EP-3 surveillance aircraft and a Chinese fighter jet and China kept the U.S. crew in detention for thirteen days. The resulting chill in U.S.-China relations continued until September 11, when the attack on the World Trade Center and the Pentagon radically shifted the administration's priorities and the war on terrorism became its centerpiece. There was no room for other enemies or a rift with China in the post-9/11 world. President Bush arbitrated the administration's internal dispute on China by siding with the engagers, although Defense Secretary Donald Rumsfeld blocked restoration of military-to-military relations for some years.

The lessons of the 1980, 1992, and 2000 campaigns were clear. In each case, an opposition candidate condemned his predecessor's policy toward China, promising to take a harder line, but once in office was forced to abandon his pledge and revert to the policy of the preceding president, with interim damage to U.S. interests and credibility. We in the Obama campaign and administration were determined to avoid these mistakes. Instead of making China a campaign issue, candidate Obama's rhetoric on China in public appearances and in written pieces was muted, firmly placing him in the mainstream of policy since Nixon. Thus President Obama took office unburdened by rash promises that he would need to walk back.

OBJECTIVES AND SYMBOLS

President Obama had a number of global foreign policy priorities that went beyond particular regions. The most important one in early 2009 was to spur global economic recovery from the financial meltdown and deep global recession of the last six months of the Bush administration. He also inherited from President Bush the challenge of halting or curtailing the Iranian and North Korean nuclear weapons programs. In addition, he wanted to end the genocide in Darfur, increase U.S. pressure on al Qaeda in Afghanistan and Pakistan, and begin to tackle the problem of climate change.

In Obama's view, China's role in all these issues was important, and in some instances critical. China was then the third largest economy in the world. If it went into recession or turned inward and closed its market, the global recession would be much deeper. As the only country with a significant relationship with North Korea, it had leverage to potentially affect the North's pursuit of nuclear weapons. China was Iran's largest trading partner and a major investor in Iran's energy sector, and therefore a player in Teheran's decisions on its future nuclear weapons program. China's large oil investments in Sudan gave it a voice in Khartoum, which to date had not been raised against the Darfur massacres but could be. And in 2009 China surpassed the United States as the world's largest emitter of greenhouse gases, with a trajectory that threatened to undo any progress the West might make in reducing emissions.

All in all, the administration's objective in the early months was to build a safety net under the U.S.-China relationship to avoid the kind of downturns that had occurred in 1981, 1989, 1993, and 2001, which would undercut cooperation on critical global issues. As an initial step, one of the first phone calls President Obama made to a foreign leader, shortly after calls to key allies in Europe and Asia, was to President Hu Jintao.

During the first few months, our team's diplomatic interactions with China dealt mostly with symbolic and process issues. The central mechanism of Bush administration interaction with China was the so-called strategic economic dialogue, headed on the U.S. side by Treasury Secretary Henry Paulson and grouping a slew of economic agencies in semi-annual delegation meetings with the Chinese. Under the guidance of then deputy secretary of state Zoellick, the two countries also held annual political and security talks at the subcabinet level. These dialogues were a sound and constructive way to build personal relationships, break down bureaucratic stovepipes (particularly within China), and permit meetings that went beyond ritualized recitation of prepared talking points.

Secretary Clinton did not wish to simply replicate the Bush model, however. She made clear from the outset that she thought the dialogues in the Bush era had failed to give enough prominence and recognition to political and security issues, and that she wished to put them on the same level as economic issues. Through dialogue with the Chinese, the administration also hoped to show how U.S. security and economic policies, as well as others like energy and climate change, were integrated and not kept in separate silos. A month of haggling ensued between State and Treasury Department officials over which of them would have the dominant role in the dialogue. Various other options, such as having Vice President Joe Biden head a unified dialogue, were considered and discarded. In early 2009 we considered the way forward at an interagency deputies' meeting that was the largest collection of officials from the largest collection of agencies that I had ever seen. Working with Deputy National Security Adviser Tom Donilon and taking into account the consensus reached in the Deputies Committee, I proposed to the Chinese that we set up a dialogue headed on the U.S. side by the secretaries of state and treasury, and on the Chinese side by the state councilor for foreign affairs (Dai Bingguo) and the vice premier overseeing the economy and finance (Wang Qishan). I suggested that they be designated special representatives of the two presidents, and that the dialogue be held annually. We were concerned that the Chinese might reject the idea because of the putative disparity in rank between a vice premier or state councilor and cabinet officials. We also wondered how China's stovepipe system would react to having two senior officials cochair a dialogue, and how to determine which half of the dialogue would handle issues such as energy and climate change. The Chinese agreed, however, and at their first meeting on April 1, 2009, in London, Presidents Obama and Hu Jintao announced the establishment of the Strategic and Economic Dialogue (S&ED), which would bring together nearly a score of officials from each side for annual meetings. This mechanism was unknown in U.S. relations with any other country in the world and therefore indicated the particular importance that the Obama administration attached to China.

The other seemingly trivial matter that we wrangled over in the first month was the Chinese request for a label for the relationship. For reasons embedded in their history and culture, the Chinese felt a deep need for a title to characterize their relations with others. Where the United States tends to concentrate on building a relationship from a base of tangible elements of cooperation, the Chinese tend to start with the overall nature of the desired relationship (as captured in a phrase) and then move toward more specific points of cooperation. China had established "strategic partnerships" with a number of countries and seemed to want a similar label for its relationship with the United States. The Bush administration had settled on the terms "constructive, cooperative, and candid" to describe the relationship, while the label we worked out with the Chinese characterized our relationship as "positive, constructive, and comprehensive." Over the ensuing years, this phrase found its way into virtually every pronouncement by senior officials, especially on the Chinese side. The ritual repetition of the phrase at every encounter triggered wry smiles from President Obama, but he understood the need to package the relationship in a way that the Chinese could sell at home.[4]

President Obama wanted to rapidly develop much more intensive interaction with Chinese leaders than had been the case in the past. To this end, Obama telephoned Hu within days after the election and the inauguration and engaged in frequent face-to-face meetings at every opportunity provided by the G-20 and G-8 conferences (often attended by President Hu), the UN General Assembly, APEC gatherings, and exchange visits in capitals. Their first direct encounter took place at the G-20 meeting in London in April 2009.[5]

Several days before the meeting, we discussed with President Obama possible travel to several Asian countries in November 2009 in connection with the annual APEC meeting in Singapore. The president indicated he felt a short visit to China at that time would make sense, and I agreed.

Immediately before that first meeting with President Hu, Obama's senior staff gathered for a briefing on possible topics of discussion. I suggested the president tell Hu of his interest in visiting China in November. Some in the room such as Secretary Clinton believed we should maintain leverage and insist on performance on a couple of issues before committing to a visit. I argued that such an approach would lead to endless wrangling, heighten mutual suspicion, and ultimately force us to drop the precondition. I had seen such bargaining over preconditions for a meeting in previous administrations and was convinced that with the Chinese, as with other serious powers, it rarely produced the desired results. The president agreed and proceeded to inform Hu of his interest in a November visit to Beijing.

At the same time, I knew the Japanese would react with dismay if they heard that the president planned to visit Beijing without visiting Tokyo first. Although we were not ready to announce a visit to Japan that had not been discussed with staff and schedulers, I called the Japanese ambassador to the United States, Ichiro Fujisaki, as soon as the Obama-Hu meeting ended to tell him to inform Tokyo that President Obama planned to visit Japan in November. Fujisaki was relieved, and Tokyo was satisfied.

In their two-hour meeting, Obama and Hu strictly followed the script. Hu Jintao rarely deviates from his talking points and did not do so on this occasion. President Obama, who liked to build on his prepared script and ad lib in the back-and-forth exchanges, did little of this during the meeting. He highlighted the need for the two sides to cooperate to roll back the North Korean nuclear program, respond to the recent North Korean missile test, halt the Iranian nuclear program, stimulate the global economy, and combat climate change. He talked of the American commitment to human rights globally and urged Hu to undertake a serious dialogue with the Dalai Lama on Tibet's future. Hu laid out familiar Chinese positions, insisting on Chinese opposition to the North Korean and Iranian nuclear weapons programs but calling on the United States to have a direct dialogue with Pyongyang and Teheran rather than rely on pressure. He laid out China's traditional approach on Taiwan, its "one China" principle, and expectation that the United States would halt sophisticated arms sales to Taiwan. There were no surprises, but the ice had been broken.

The Chinese proposed that the two sides issue a joint statement or communiqué marking the event. We had no desire to do so, given the history of political controversy sparked by joint communiqués focusing on the Taiwan issue. Instead we agreed to issue parallel (and identical) unilateral press statements that contained an anodyne comment on Taiwan.

A decision that had to be made at this early stage was who was to be the ambassador to China. In April presidential personnel approached me for ideas, since their original efforts to identify a qualified, prominent, and willing candidate had not borne fruit. I said one person they might consider was Jon Huntsman Jr., whom I characterized as a "Hail Mary" and was a good friend from the time we worked together at the Office of the U.S. Trade Representative (USTR). I described him as a moderate Republican accustomed to working across the partisan divide, a fluent speaker of Chinese from his days as a Mormon missionary in Taiwan, a potential future presidential candidate, a former ambassador to Singapore considered for Beijing by George W. Bush's administration, and a thoroughly decent man and a patriot. As the governor of Utah, he was enjoying an 85 percent favorable rating. Although I saw very little chance of his leaving his current post in Salt Lake City, I thought perhaps it was worth a try.

The next day, I was told that the president wanted me to call Huntsman to sound him out. I did so. Jon laughed and said he had a good job already but still asked me to make my pitch, which I did. The day after that, Jon called back to say he was intrigued. Over the next few days, he spoke to White House chief of staff Rahm Emanuel several times and finally to the president and ultimately decided to take the job.[6]

Jon was an excellent ambassador. He understood well the difference in the roles of Washington policymakers and an ambassador. As a result, he was not only one of the administration's most effective ambassadors in the Asia-Pacific region but also one of the easiest for Washington to deal with. He was the same pragmatic, cooperative team player I had known at the USTR, unburdened by an ego or a compulsion to monopolize the spotlight.

When stories broke in December 2010 that Jon was considering running for president in 2012, I was surprised, as I had assumed he would wait until 2016 before doing so.[7] His last four months in office after the story of his possible candidacy leaked created discomfort in the West Wing, though President Obama remained relaxed about the situation, simply asking Jon to concentrate exclusively on his job until his tenure ended. Jon understood the awkwardness and ultimately decided to leave Beijing several months earlier than he had intended so that he could test the Republican primary waters. Regardless of the unusual ending to his tour, U.S.-China relations were well served by Huntsman's stewardship, and I never heard misgivings or regrets from the president concerning the appointment.

FOUR

NORTH KOREA: BREAKING THE PATTERN

UPON TAKING OFFICE, the Obama administration knew that its biggest challenge in East Asia, besides getting the relationship with China right, was to devise a strategy for dealing with a nuclear North Korea. The North's nuclear weapons program had been a large concern of the previous three administrations.

Under George H. W. Bush, all U.S. nuclear weapons were withdrawn from South Korea, paving the way for a North-South agreement in 1992 that banned the manufacture, deployment, or use of nuclear weapons. When North Korea proceeded with its nuclear program nonetheless and a crisis arose in 1993–94 over the North's threat to withdraw from the Nuclear Nonproliferation Treaty (NPT) and to end inspections by the International Atomic Energy Agency (IAEA), President Bill Clinton negotiated the Agreed Framework in 1994, which essentially froze and promised to end North Korea's plutonium program for producing weapons-grade material in return for support by the United States, Japan, and South Korea for the construction of two light-water reactors to produce electric power and for other assistance.

The administration of George W. Bush was profoundly skeptical of the Agreed Framework. Some in his administration believed that anything short of regime change in Pyongyang was a poor stopgap at best. Many thought that North Korea would find a way to continue its nuclear weapons program despite the agreement's inspection provisions, as was confirmed by intelligence indicating that North Korea was undertaking a uranium enrichment program, an alternative means of producing weapons-grade material, outside the watchful eyes of IAEA inspectors. In 2002 the State Department's assistant secretary for East Asia, Jim Kelly, confronted the North Koreans over their uranium enrichment program. They responded angrily with a statement suggesting it was true. The United States then halted fuel deliveries and suspended work on the light-water reactors promised to the North. Shortly after, the North withdrew from the NPT and IAEA, threw out the inspectors, and resumed operations at the Yongbyon plutonium facilities.[1]

The next five years saw twists and turns in Bush administration policy and uneven progress by the North toward the development of its nuclear program. Washington and Beijing worked out a mechanism for Six-Party Talks among China, Japan, North Korea, South Korea, Russia, and the United States. In September 2005, the parties issued a joint statement in which North Korea agreed to a staged elimination of "all nuclear weapons and existing nuclear programs" and to return "at an early date" to the NPT and to IAEA safeguards. In response, the United States agreed to work toward normalized relations with North Korea, provide it with security assurances, and take the lead in providing heavy fuel oil to satisfy North Korea's energy needs.

In the immediate wake of the 2005 joint statement, and seemingly in a manner not fully coordinated within the U.S. government, Washington froze North Korean accounts in a bank in Macau, Banco Delta Asia, believing it was a primary means for North Korean international proliferation activity and money laundering. This action stung the North Korean leadership, freezing assets near and dear to them. In response, the North launched a Taepodong-2 (TPD-2) intercontinental ballistic missile (ICBM) test in July 2006 and detonated a nuclear device for the first time three months later. In 2007, after difficult negotiations, the two sides agreed on reciprocal steps and a resumption of negotiations. North Korea consented to shut down and eventually seal the Yongbyon nuclear reactor and to allow the return of IAEA inspectors. It agreed to a phased disabling and ultimate dismantling of the entire Yongbyon facility. Although nuclear weapons were not directly addressed in either of the two documents drawn up in 2007, it was understood that elimination of the North Korean nuclear weapons stockpile would be the last step in the process and be a condition of U.S.

recognition, security guarantees, and foreign economic assistance. If North Korea complied, the United States would resume heavy fuel oil shipments, remove North Korea from the list of state sponsors of terrorism, drop the sanctions covered by the Trading with the Enemy Act, and unfreeze the North's assets in Banco Delta Asia.

When the Obama administration assumed office, the architect of the 2005 and 2007 agreements with North Korea, Assistant Secretary of State Chris Hill, was still in place pending confirmation of his replacement, Kurt Campbell. Many of us admired Hill's perseverance in making some, albeit limited, progress toward the North's denuclearization in an administration hostile to him personally and toward his diplomacy. Our team assumed the six-party process would continue. But the consensus both within the Obama administration and within the intelligence community was that North Korea was determined to maintain its nuclear weapons program, regardless of its commitments.

At the outset, the administration sought to reconcile several competing objectives:

—Recommit to the goal of complete, irreversible, and verifiable denuclearization of North Korea. Anything less would be problematic for the United States, of course, but even more so for North Korea's neighbors, Japan and South Korea, which would remain under the threat of a nuclear-armed North Korea in any other scenario.

—Halt North Korea's proliferation of nuclear materials, ballistic missiles, and technology. The North had provided assistance for construction of a nuclear facility in Syria, blown up by the Israelis in 2007, and there were reports of other forms of proliferation to rogue states.

—Until such time as the North's stockpile could be eliminated, freeze and degrade its existing programs.

—Use diplomatic channels to achieve much more intense coordination with America's allies, especially with South Korea. Under the Bush administration, there was a strong perception in Tokyo and Seoul that the United States was working more closely with China and saving drive-by consultations with them until after the fact. Holding adequate consultations with Seoul and Tokyo had been problematic under Bush, in part because Hill's negotiating team operated in secrecy to avoid being picked apart by internal adversaries led by Vice President Cheney, but also because Japan's government took a very hard line on North Korea while South Korea permitted excessive accommodation of Pyongyang.

Responding to a question in a Democratic primaries debate, candidate Obama had suggested a readiness to meet with America's adversaries, including Kim Jong-il. The statement was designed to differentiate his potential administration from a Bush presidency that seemed predisposed to seeing the world in terms of good and evil and thereby missed opportunities to mitigate conflicts. But it went too far in accepting the questioner's premise that Obama would be prepared to accept such a meeting in his first year in office. Critics made the statement into a sort of Obama doctrine. I myself was uncomfortable with the statement, feeling it lacked the nuance that Obama normally conveyed. So were others in the foreign policy team. During my time in office, I never heard the statement reiterated in any form, suggesting that, as I had assumed, it was meant to convey tactical flexibility under the right circumstances, not an intention to chase after dictators. Clarification came in his inaugural address, when Obama said he was prepared to reach his hand out to adversaries if they reciprocated, which he in fact did subsequently with the leaders of Burma when they took steps to improve human rights conditions in their country.[2]

In the midafternoon of my first day in office, before our team had had a chance to consider in depth a possible way forward on Korea, I received a cable from the State Department asking for clearance by 4 p.m. It contained an oral message from Secretary Clinton "to the people of North Korea." Its talking points focused mainly on the policy pursued by the Bush administration in its final weeks, so as to provide the North Koreans with a sense of continuity in policy. I assumed that Secretary Clinton had not seen the draft.

I called one of assistant secretary Hill's deputies responsible for Korea and unleashed a verbal barrage, reminding him that a new president had been inaugurated only the previous day. I added, unnecessarily but pointedly, that I had no intention of barging into the Oval Office on the president's first day to get him to sign off on such a message, which could not go out otherwise. The new president and the new national security team, I pointed out, deserved a chance to consider the direction we were going in before the bureaucracy attempted to tie us to existing processes and policies. Henceforth, I added, we would not communicate with the North Koreans without first coordinating with Seoul, Tokyo, and ideally with Beijing and Moscow. The message was stopped.[3]

North Korea Launches a Satellite, Sort Of

In February the intelligence community reported that North Korea was preparing to test another Taepodong-2, probably loaded with a satellite so that the test could be characterized as a satellite launch rather than a ballistic missile test. The distinction was important in order for North Korea to claim that it was not violating the UN Security Council resolution of 2006, adopted after the first TPD-2 test, banning all ballistic missile tests, whatever their purpose. But in fact the rocket used to launch a satellite is no different from the one used for a weapons payload. Whatever the North Koreans planned to call the test was irrelevant. It was a ballistic missile test. What made the intent all the more clear was that North Korea had at best rudimentary satellite production capability. As one of our intelligence analysts put it, the North Koreans may as well have been launching a refrigerator as a functioning satellite.

We convened frequent Deputies Committee meetings to consider how to deal with the prospective North Korean missile test, while also faced with escalating rhetoric from the North in February 2009 blaming the United States for stalling the Six-Party Talks. We urged the Chinese and the Russians to press the North Koreans to halt their preparations for the test. We also considered a range of military options to deal with the highly unlikely contingency that the North's missile might be equipped with a warhead and be aimed at American territory. It was believed that if the test was successful, Hawaii might conceivably be in its range. We positioned antiballistic missile assets to ensure the safety of American territory.[4] The State Department told Pyongyang that if the North Koreans decided to forgo the launch, its special representative for Korea, Steve Bosworth, could go ahead with a visit to the North, but if they did not cancel the test, he could not. Our team decided to suspend discussions about the next stage in implementing the disablement of Yongbyon's plutonium facility. It seemed unthinkable to proceed with the further concessions required in the disablement process when North Korea was being disdainful of its obligations regarding ballistic missile testing.

In March the president chaired a National Security Council meeting in which the political and military contingencies were considered and responses decided upon. He made clear that Strategic Command and Pacific Command had the necessary authority to defend U.S. territory should a threat present itself.

The president told his senior staff he wanted a policy to break the cycle of provocation, extortion, and reward that various U.S. administrations had confronted and ultimately accommodated in the past fifteen years. The United States, he said, should behave in ways that threw the North Koreans off their game plan and that presented them with unwelcome surprises. Defense Secretary Robert Gates stressed the importance of not providing inducements to bring North Korea back to the table, or "not paying for the same horse three times." The president agreed. There was no mention then, or at any subsequent time, of candidate Obama's suggestion of a willingness to meet Kim Jong-il.

The North Koreans proceeded with their test on April 5. The first two phases of the three-stage rocket performed well, and the rocket traveled more than 2,000 miles across the Pacific. The third stage quickly failed, and the launch of the "satellite" failed as well. The North Koreans triumphantly announced the success of the satellite launch, indeed claiming it was broadcasting North Korean anthems. But they failed to provide the frequency for the nonexistent satellite broadcasts.

The NSC team decided to seek UN Security Council action to condemn the launch. The Chinese, supported by the Russians, opposed any action. At first their representatives argued, half-heartedly, that it was indeed a satellite launch, or was claimed to be such, and therefore was arguably outside the parameters of the UN resolution banning ballistic missile tests. In contrast to its launch behavior in 2006, this time, as part of its effort to claim legitimacy for a "civilian launch," the North acceded to an international treaty governing uses of space and notified the International Civil Aviation Organization (ICAO) and the International Maritime Organization (IMO) of its intended launch. The Japanese pushed for a resolution of condemnation, considering anything less inadequate. The U.S. ambassador to the United Nations, Susan Rice, ultimately persuaded the Chinese and Russians to accept a Security Council presidential statement, rather than a resolution. The presidential statement explicitly condemned the launch and made clear that whether it was a satellite launch or not did not matter under the applicable UN resolution (Resolution 1718, passed in 2006 after North Korea's first nuclear test): it was banned in any event. This was an important step in closing the satellite loophole that the North Koreans had sought to exploit. It also strengthened the U.S. government's hand by demonstrating that the Chinese and Russians were on board with the United States in resisting North Korean fudging on its obligations.

Negotiation of the resolution was complicated by an overaggressive performance by Japan's ambassador to the United Nations, who publicly demanded a resolution rather than a presidential statement and leaked reports critical of the United States for accepting less. The Japanese had argued that a weak resolution was better than a strong presidential statement, a view shared by no other UN Security Council members. The United States ultimately secured a strong statement, the Japanese concurred, and the statement was issued on April 13, 2009.[5]

On the other hand, our policy team coordinated closely and effectively with the South Koreans. Secretary Clinton's visit to Seoul in February 2009 had opened the door to a warm relationship with South Korea's new president, Lee Myung-bak. He wanted to pursue a tougher policy toward the North than his predecessor, Roh Moo-hyun, demanding reciprocity instead of offering one-sided concessions. He had terminated food assistance to the North and made it clear that he expected North Korea to address Seoul's concerns about nuclear weapons before it could expect aid. He was anxious to work with President Obama, and his approach seemed to mesh well with the president's.

In response to the Security Council statement, the North Koreans announced that they were once again expelling the IAEA inspectors and removing the seals and cameras monitoring the Yongbyon reactor. They claimed this was in retaliation for the UN action.

The sequence of events suggests strongly that the North Koreans planned all along to proceed with a series of provocations in the first half of 2009, including the missile test, the expulsion of the inspectors, the halting of the Six-Party Talks, and testing of a second nuclear device. They were repeating their old pattern of provocation designed to induce a reward. Our national security team was determined not to provide a reward.

In April the North Koreans sent Washington a private message making several threats: (1) to explode a nuclear device, (2) to develop an

ICBM capable of reaching the United States, (3) to enrich uranium to enable them to develop a light-water reactor. They revealed these warnings publicly. We also suspected that they would seek to proliferate nuclear technology abroad.[6] The administration responded with a strong warning about the consequences of each and shared its concerns with the other members of the six parties. The White House also issued a public statement that reiterated President George W. Bush's 2006 warning that the United States would hold North Korea fully responsible for any proliferation. To address Japan and South Korea's concerns that Washington might be focused too exclusively on the proliferation threat, a statement was added indicating that the United States would defend its allies.[7]

Secretary Clinton called me one morning in March 2009 to suggest that the United States should be more reserved about our interest in the continuation of Six-Party Talks. In her view, constant reiteration of the importance of returning to talks was conveying a sense of desperation and undercutting U.S. leverage. With a more reserved approach, she felt the Chinese, who regarded the Six-Party Talks as their major diplomatic achievement, would feel a greater sense of urgency about persuading North Korea to undertake serious actions toward denuclearization. I agreed with her. Henceforth, the administration's public enthusiasm for Six-Party Talks was much more muted, noting their potential utility but emphasizing they were only a means to an end, not a goal in themselves. As our team put it, we were not interested in "talks for the sake of talks." Through this adjustment, the administration made clear to the North Koreans, the Chinese, and the Russians, not only that it would not pay for a resumption of talks, but that much more was needed from the North before any such dialogue could resume.

To enhance the message of North Korea's isolation and U.S. attention to the situation, President Obama decided to meet with South Korean president Lee Myung-bak on the margins of the London G-20 meeting. Before the April 2 meeting, I told the president that we had scheduled a photo op, without microphones, at the beginning so that Lee could highlight his relationship with Obama for those back home. While the video was rolling, Obama called an audible, as he would say, and told the journalists he had a few comments he wanted them to record. To the surprise and delight of President Lee, he then delivered a two-minute picture- and tone-perfect paean to the U.S.–South Korea alliance, filled with details about the relationship and our military commitment. In the meeting, the president invited Lee to visit Washington in June.

He was one of the first foreign head-of-state visitors, and he was treated specially. While the White House was not yet hosting state visits because of the dissonance of such events at a time of economic recession, a lunch was held for Lee in the East Wing, followed by a joint press conference with President Obama in the Rose Garden and a one-on-one forty-five-minute conversation with the president in the breakfast room off the Oval Office. The public and private messages indicated solidarity against North Korea's nuclear program and other provocations and the firmness of the U.S. security guarantee to South Korea. Presidents Obama and Lee hit it off very well, with Obama commenting afterward that this was someone Washington could work closely with. But just as pressure on North Korea was ratcheting up and U.S. diplomacy was highlighting its solidarity with its allies, a distracting sideshow was becoming an unwelcome diversion and risked sending contrary signals.

INNOCENTS ABROAD:
AMERICAN JOURNALISTS JAILED IN NORTH KOREA

On March 17 two American journalists working for Al Gore's cable network, Current TV, Laura Ling and Euna Lee, stumbled across the North Korean border while working on a documentary on North Korean refugees in China. They were spotted by North Korean border guards and captured while attempting to flee back into China. Reports indicated that they had substantial material including names of dissidents and human rights activists stored on their digital equipment, which fell into North Korean hands.[8] Our team knew immediately that the North Koreans would hold the journalists and use them for leverage on political and security issues before considering their release, probably when a senior U.S. politician was dispatched to pick them up (such was their history). We were determined not to accept North Korean extortion and its linkage to other issues.

I briefed the president the day the incident occurred, noting that their male photographer had outrun them and the guards and made it back safely onto Chinese territory. One of the president's aides, Chief of Staff Rahm Emanuel, wondered aloud whether the photographer's chivalry book was printed backwards. This reminded the president of the story about the fellow confronted by a charging bear who told his colleague they should run. His partner replied, "Why? We can't outrun the bear." The fellow answered, "I don't have to outrun the bear, just you." He shook his head in disbelief, and asked how we should and could deal with the situation. I said there was a history of releases of Americans from North Korea in response to high-level visitors, and we should expect such a pattern to repeat in a few months, but not before the journalists were tried and convicted. He said he wanted us to monitor the situation and keep him informed.

Over the next few months, we maintained contact with the North Koreans through a variety of channels, demanding release of the journalists. We secured access to the women through our diplomatic protecting power in Pyongyang, the Swedish ambassador, who kept us posted on their status and health and brought them needed medicine.

As expected, a number of political figures offered themselves as visitors to Pyongyang to seek their release. Among them were former President Jimmy Carter, Governor Bill Richardson of New Mexico, and Senator John Kerry of Massachusetts (Kerry was the most circumspect of the three, and the one most clearly anxious to avoid complicating U.S policy objectives with regard to North Korea). There was no need to seriously consider any of them, since the North Koreans showed no signs to anyone that they were prepared to release the journalists. In the meantime, they conducted a trial, in North Korean style, and sentenced the women to eight years of hard labor.

Washington told the North Koreans in May that it was prepared to allow Al Gore to travel to Pyongyang to pick up the journalists if they agreed. Gore seemed like a logical choice to us, since he was the founder of Current TV and the journalists' employer. The North Koreans refused to consider Gore. Instead, they proposed that Bill Clinton go.

Deputy National Security Adviser Tom Donilon, Director of National Intelligence Dennis Blair, my Korea deputy Danny Russel, and I were opposed to sending Clinton. We felt the North Koreans would treat his arrival as a kind of state visit, with cheering, synchronized card-performing masses, dancing girls with ribbons, massive publicity, and a banquet. We felt the North Koreans could see it as a political reward. We also felt it could encourage further hostage-taking by the North and detract from our negotiating firmness in a way that would undercut our strategy on the nuclear issues. Reactions in Seoul and Tokyo were another concern. In addition, we were uneasy about the idea of the secretary of state's spouse going to North Korea on such a mission.

We met with the president, presenting him with competing views. Thinking along the same lines as I did, he declined to send Bill Clinton at that time.

Pressure continued to build to resolve the matter. The State Department was in regular contact with the journalists' parents, who had agreed to keep a low profile for the sake of a quiet resolution, but their patience was running out. Before long, they were likely to go public with a campaign, against not only the North Koreans but also against the Obama administration. One of the prisoners, Laura Ling, was the sister of Lisa Ling, a prominent television journalist, and the American media were expected to be manipulated by the North Koreans to build sympathy for whatever demands they were making to secure the women's release. Al Gore was pressing the president as well.

Secretary Clinton was particularly concerned that the journalists might continue to be detained even after being assured of their release as part of a deal involving a visit by her husband. We would soon be steamrollered by a public campaign, she argued, and it would be hard to justify why we had decided not to send Bill. She therefore proposed that Bill Clinton go to Pyongyang on a single-issue humanitarian mission to bring back the journalists. National Security Adviser Jim Jones concurred with her, as did Deputy Secretary James Steinberg. I still disagreed. But it was decided that we should go back to the North Koreans with an offer to send Bill Clinton on the condition that it would be a brief twenty-four-hour visit, with no publicity or journalists invited, no large banquet, no welcoming ceremony, and above all an ironclad guarantee of the journalists' release.

The North Koreans agreed to our proposal. We briefed former president Clinton, who said he viewed the decision on whether he should go as a close call. He fully understood the risks to our policy objectives and readily agreed to our suggestions about how he should comport himself. I warned him of the likelihood of an unwelcome invitation to a stadium event, and Kurt Campbell recommended that he "channel his inner Dick Cheney" and look as dour as possible whenever there were cameras around. We gave him no message, oral or written, to carry from President

Obama, nor did we provide U.S. government personnel or support for the mission, which he undertook on a privately chartered aircraft. We made it clear to the North Koreans that the former president was coming solely on a humanitarian mission to bring home the journalists, not to negotiate. We also gave Seoul and Tokyo notice of the visit, assuring them there would be no negotiations.

During his August 4–5 visit, Clinton conducted himself in exemplary fashion, avoiding the risks we had worried about. At dinner, for example, when Kim Jong-il invited him to a "special performance" at a nearby stadium—a synchronized card display with a crowd of 100,000 turned out especially for the visitor—Clinton pretended three times not to hear Kim. When one of Kim's aides tried to press the matter further, Kim said, "Don't worry, I can give away the tickets."

Bill Clinton brought the journalists home with apparent minimal damage to our larger equities. We all felt a sense of relief that the journalists, who had been mistreated, were safe and sound. We also felt considerable irritation at American innocents abroad who stumble into such situations as if they were in downtown Los Angeles and then expect to be saved, without regard to the damage they do to U.S. national interests. The possibility of repeat performances by other gullible or misguided Americans, putting us in a similar box, worried us, and rightly so, although subsequent incidents did not involve as "valuable" a prize as Ling and Lee were.[9]

A VISIT TO NORTHEAST ASIA TO CHANGE BEIJING'S SECURITY CALCULUS

On May 25, two months after the American journalists were captured, the North Koreans exploded a second underground nuclear device. With Pyongyang clearly embarked on a new round of provocations and further ballistic missile tests in the offing, the administration felt it had to do something to change perceptions and actions, particularly in Beijing.

Deputy Secretary of State Steinberg, whose experience with and understanding of China was unmatched in the administration, argued persuasively that the Chinese would be unlikely to put sufficient pressure on Pyongyang unless they calculated that North Korean behavior was affecting their own security interests. He proposed that we send a delegation to

Beijing (and Seoul and Tokyo) to share our analysis of the impact of North Korea's conduct. The basic framework of the presentation was that North Korea's continuing provocations had brought Washington to an "inflection point." If North Korea's nuclear weapons and intercontinental ballistic missile programs continued and ended in deployments, it would inevitably cause the United States and its allies to alter their security posture to respond to the emerging threat. A North Korea with a growing nuclear arsenal and the means of delivering warheads would alter the calculations and plans of the allies to counter it. U.S. military deployments in the western Pacific would increase to counter the growing threat. Missile defense systems with the intent of ensuring America could not be targeted would be significantly expanded. While this missile defense capability would not be aimed at degrading China's modest nuclear deterrent force, it would inevitably have some effect in that regard. The United States, South Korea, and Japan would explore collectively and individually other means of defense. Doctrines of preemption, bruited about in Japan, would gain greater force. While the United States opposed the emergence of new nuclear powers, the North Korean program would strengthen the hand of those in favor of developing nuclear weapons in both Japan and South Korea.

I briefed the president on the delegation's proposed mission and message to get his blessing. He nodded, "What you'll be telling the Chinese is not a threat. It's simply reality." He contacted Hu Jintao to tell him of our impending visit to ensure that it received attention.

In early June 2009, Steinberg and I, along with the special representative for North Korea policy, Stephen W. Bosworth, and representatives of the Defense Department and intelligence community, set out for Beijing. We visited Seoul and Tokyo en route, which both indicated strong support for the message. In Beijing, we were received by State Councilor Dai Bingguo, Foreign Minister Yang Jiechi, and other senior officials. As usual, there was little immediate response as the Chinese listened and absorbed our message.

Eventually, however, our visit and discussions bore fruit. We worked closely with the Chinese and Russians to pass a UN Security Council resolution that imposed the most draconian sanctions ever placed on North Korea. Among its provisions were an embargo on arms exports and a nearly total embargo on arms imports, sanctions against financial transactions that could aid North Korea's programs for weapons of mass destruction (WMD), a procedure for inspecting ships that might be carrying North Korean arms, and restrictions on companies doing business with North Korea's arms industry.[10]

None of us in the Deputies Committee, which was meeting regularly to consider North Korea policy, felt that this new sanctions regime would induce the North to suddenly change course. But we did believe that the more stringent measures would hurt. They would reverse the pattern of tolerating North Korea's provocations and present Pyongyang with a starker choice: end your nuclear program if you wish to gain international acceptance and assistance or face ever-increasing pressure.

Over the next couple of years the sanctions regime, reinforced by subsequent tightening, did indeed make it more difficult for North Korea to earn foreign currency for its nuclear and weapons programs, not to mention luxury goods for the leadership. Sending illicit goods abroad also became more complicated, since shipments were at risk of inspection and seizure. In a number of instances, countries including Thailand and the United Arab Emirates seized North Korean arms shipments that violated the UN resolution. Exposed to tracking by the U.S. Navy, North Korean ships believed to be en route to Burma with arms were unable to make their deliveries and forced to turn around.[11]

These measures were not intended to further deprive the long-suffering North Korean people. The country's economy already was in a shambles, now bereft of South Korean assistance as well. Rather the goal was to help concentrate the minds of the North Korean leadership. While it is true they have shown little compunction about risking mass starvation in the past in order to continue their WMD programs, they also on occasion have been compelled to freeze or slow their WMD programs in order to persuade foreign donors to open their purses. The Obama administration hoped over time to affect their calculus and to make them understand that their continued pursuit of a nuclear weapons program would damage their personal interests.

1) Increasing Sanctions against the DPRK was not intended to hurt the people of the DPRK was to concentrate the mind of the DPRK leaders

FIVE

JAPAN:
FROM LDP TO DPJ RULE

WHEN BARACK OBAMA took office, relations with Japan did not seem to present serious problems that would preoccupy senior officials. The Liberal Democratic Party (LDP), headed by veteran politician Taro Aso, was still in power after a fifty-year hold, except for a break of one year. We wanted to strengthen Tokyo's confidence in our commitment to the alliance and common view of security in the Asia-Pacific region. Given the long history of U.S. cooperation with the LDP, this did not seem an especially daunting challenge.

Several factors, however, signaled that special efforts were needed with the Japanese. For one thing, the LDP has had a history of some friction with America's Democratic presidents over what it sees as their susceptibility to trade protectionism and uncertain degree of commitment to the alliance. Much of the Japanese press has a zero-sum approach to American officials, seeing them either as pro-Japanese (and therefore trustworthy allies) or pro-Chinese (and therefore adversaries). In the press's simplistic analytic framework, I was identified as a presumed problem because of my background in relations with China.[1]

Another challenge was the legacy of several years of chafing between the State Department's East Asia Bureau and the Japanese government, which judged Assistant Secretary Chris Hill's consultations on North Korea to be inadequate. Kurt Campbell, who was in line to succeed Hill, was well known and respected in Japan for his work in the Defense Department in the 1990s, but his confirmation was delayed until June, during which time the administration needed to start building a solid base for the relationship.

As noted earlier, Washington took two opportunities to do so: Hillary Clinton's first step on foreign soil as secretary of state was in Japan in February; and the first foreign head of government that President Obama received in the Oval Office was Taro Aso, also in February. With the Japanese, symbols like the timing of these visits is often more important than substance. The decision to jump Japan to the front of the line was well received in Tokyo.

The only difficult issue on our policy team's initial agenda was the plan to move the Futenma Marine Corps Air Station from the crowded city of Ginowan in Okinawa to a less crowded location on the island. It was part of a broader plan to reduce the U.S. military footprint in Okinawa by removing 8,000 marines and their 9,000 dependents and sending them to Guam, thus keeping them in the Western Pacific theater but reducing a source of tension in Okinawa. The plan had been developed in the mid-1990s, but was not yet implemented because of seemingly endless disputes among local Okinawa residents and politicians, Tokyo, and Washington over the plan's details. Questions such as the shape of the runway, possible landfill in the harbor, the need for an environmental impact study, the source and amount of financing required to house marines moved to Guam, and so on kept half a generation of U.S. and Japanese military officers busy, but without any groundbreaking solutions. No one was especially enamored of the agreed-upon result, the so-called Futenma Replacement Facility, although most of those who had studied the matter considered it better than all the alternatives.

During her February visit to Guam, Secretary Clinton signed the Guam International Agreement, under which the Japanese consented to provide funding for the move to Guam. DPJ kingpin Ichiro Ozawa made headlines just before Clinton's arrival by condemning the marines' presence in Okinawa, but that did not seem to portend early problems.

Through a series of domestic policy mishaps, some caused by Aso and some by his predecessors, LDP popularity went into a free fall in the first half of 2009. When I briefed President Obama before his February 2009 meeting with Aso, I noted that whereas the president's popularity rating in Japan was at 90 percent, Aso's was only 10 percent. By late spring, expert consensus was that the opposition Democratic Party of Japan

(DPJ) would win a sweeping victory. Indeed, it routed the LDP in a land-slide in the late August elections, and Yukio Hatoyama, the son of a for-mer LDP foreign minister and grandson of a former prime minister and founder of the LDP, was selected as prime minister.

Some of the positions advocated by the DPJ and rhetoric used by their spokesmen during the campaign caused unease in Washington. I met with several parliamentarians and DPJ staff over the summer before the elec-tion and listened to their perspectives. They spoke of their support for the alliance but also offered criticism of U.S. policies in Afghanistan, Iran, and North Korea, suggesting that they could pick and choose where they would stand with the United States. They also hinted at a desire to "find a better balance" between China and the United States in Japan's external relations, and to diminish Japanese dependence on the United States. Some were skeptical about the U.S. military presence in Okinawa and made reference to a DPJ campaign pledge to revisit the Futenma Replace-ment Facility plan.

The president publicly embraced Prime Minister Hatoyama, giving him no cause for unease about the U.S. tie. Obama called him to con-gratulate him and met him in New York a few weeks after Hatoyama assumed office, making a strong statement in front of the cameras wel-coming the change that the prime minister represented and that the peo-ple of Japan wanted.[2] Indeed, five decades of LDP rule had left the polit-ical and economic system in stagnation, unable to solve or even address the problems that had overtaken Japan beginning around 1990. The hope throughout the country as well as among Japan-watchers in the United States was that the DPJ would unleash a new spirit of reform and dynamism. Our people assumed there would be at least some minor tur-bulence on the foreign policy side, partly because of the DPJ's contempt for the professional bureaucracy protective of the U.S.-Japan alliance. But the DPJ certainly did not win with a mandate to undo the alliance or sig-nificantly alter the relationship with the United States, so we felt we could ride out any problems.

The early weeks of the Hatoyama cabinet, however, produced a num-ber of disturbing developments. First, it reiterated Hatoyama's campaign position on renegotiating the Futenma Replacement Facility agreement to find a solution that removed all U.S. Marines from Okinawa. Along with many of my National Security Council and State Department colleagues,

I had thought this stance would be modified once Hatoyama confronted the realities of governing, Japan's defense requirements, and the lack of good alternatives. On the contrary, the position seemed to be enduring.

Second, Hatoyama made a number of unwelcome public comments suggesting that he wanted Japan to have a more "balanced" foreign policy, that is, to be "less dependent" on the United States and more tilted toward China. Our Asia experts had been unconcerned about the prospect of improved Sino-Japanese relations. Indeed, we welcomed such a change. Rising tensions between these historic rivals would have consequences for global and regional peace and make it difficult for the United States to maintain good relations with China while remaining true to its alliance with Japan. Rapprochement after the Sino-Japanese tensions of 2006— when Chinese protesters attacked Japanese diplomatic and commercial establishments in response to a visit by Japan's prime minister to a shrine where Japanese war criminals from World War II are memorialized—was a good development from the U.S. perspective. But talk of "balance" between the United States, Japan's most important ally, and China was a different matter. In December 2009, as if to demonstrate the direction in which the DPJ wished to go, Ichiro Ozawa led a delegation of some 150 Japanese parliamentarians plus another 300 businessmen to China to call on Hu Jintao and begin a new era in Sino-Japanese relations. Hu shook hands with several hundred of them to show his appreciation.[3]

Third, the DPJ cabinet floated ideas that would have reversed decades of U.S. nuclear doctrine and shaken the alliance. The foreign minister publicly called on the United States to renounce first use of nuclear weapons in the event of conflict, a long-standing pillar of U.S. deterrence and defense of Japan. The cabinet also began investigating the history of U.S. agreements with LDP governments that permitted the stationing and transit of nuclear-armed U.S. vessels in Japan.

Fourth, and perhaps most troubling, Hatoyama announced his support for a so-called East Asia Community composed of the principal countries of Asia. One of a number of proposals for new overarching pan-Asian institutions, Hatoyama's idea would have excluded the United States from the community. Back in the 1990s, Malaysia's anti-American prime minister Mahathir had advocated the creation of an Asia-only East Asian Caucus, but the United States, spearheaded by then secretary of state Jim Baker, resisted this proposal, as did its key Asian allies, and the idea failed

Prime Minister Yukio Hotoyama, representing the Japanese Democratic Party, proposed in 2009 an East Asia Community with US excluded. Thus pan Asian proposal upset the Vietnamese which did not want to be in any organization to get traction. The thought that America's closest ally in Asia should be pursuing a similar proposal was astonishing to the Obama administration.

Asian leaders were equally astounded. When Hatoyama laid out the suggestion to the East Asia Summit meeting in October 2009, the president of Vietnam expressed deep concern to one of America's regional allies, asking him to help kill this dangerous idea. Vietnam of course was concerned that the proposed structure would place its historical adversary China at the center of East Asia institution building without an American balance. The irony that Vietnam, of all countries, should have understood the strategic foolishness of such a proposal while America's strongest ally in the region did not was not lost on anyone. Friends in Australia, Singapore, South Korea, and Indonesia, among others, made clear they regarded this idea as unacceptable.

By the time President Obama launched his first Asian trip in November with a stop in Japan, it was clear to me that the Hatoyama government was strategically incoherent. Our Asia team was getting conflicting advice from the Japan experts we spoke to about how to proceed. Those committed to the historic U.S.-Japan relationship and used to alliance management through the LDP urged the administration to stand firm, not only privately but also publicly. On the other hand, Japan-watchers who were long-time critics of the LDP told us to show patience, and some even suggested walking away from the Futenma agreement.

A month earlier, Defense Secretary Robert Gates had visited Japan, and the tensions over Okinawa were already in evidence. While Gates did not seek a public confrontation, he was firm with Japanese officials in private about the need to go ahead with the Futenma Replacement Facility plan without further changes. However, Japanese officials leaked the transcript of Gates's meeting with the foreign minister, and Washington was suddenly faced with a public showdown over Okinawa.[4] Japan-watchers who were sympathetic with the DPJ inundated me with calls demanding that the administration distance itself from Gates's supposedly confrontational policy.

Obama was determined not to allow the Okinawa issue to dominate his visit. He wanted it to be about the strength of the U.S.-Japan alliance and its global and regional importance. These were the central themes of his public speech and his comments at the joint press conference with Hatoyama.[5] In the private dinner hosted by the prime minister, however,

Obama was more direct. He made it clear that the situation in Asia required that Japan and the United States reaffirm the centrality of the alliance and that they could not do that while squabbling over Okinawa bases. Hatoyama explained that he was committed to lightening the burden imposed on the people of Okinawa by U.S. bases, and he hoped for understanding on the part of the United States, ending with the words, "Trust me" on this. Obama said he trusted him. By making the matter personal, and a question of trust between heads of government, Hatoyama seemed to be saying don't worry, I will make the Okinawa issue come out fine.

Before the joint press conference, the president asked me how I would answer an expected question about the Futenma Replacement Facility. I suggested he talk about how important it was for Japan to "fully implement" the Futenma Replacement agreement, rather than getting into a defense of the specifics of the agreement or a critique of Hatoyama for his resistance. I felt that it was important for the president not to undercut Gates's message, and that this was the best way to do so without confronting Hatoyama. The president agreed and used this line as part of a thoughtful reply about the firmness of the alliance.

The entire press corps understood the president's remarks and reported that he had stood by Gates's message—with one exception. On November 13 the *New York Times* ran a front-page story accusing the president of running away from Gates and undercutting him. After a series of furious e-mails from Press Secretary Bob Gibbs at the White House, the *Times* retracted the story.

In the following days, Hatoyama set for himself a deadline to have the Okinawa problem resolved by the end of the year, but he failed to meet it. For Obama's part, he projected patience, saying he was not seeking deadlines but decisions that would hold. The Japanese public began turning decisively against Hatoyama, as reflected in his plummeting poll numbers not long after he assumed office. He and his cabinet soon stopped talking about rebalancing between China and the United States and instead emphasized the alliance. There was no more talk of an America-free East Asia Community. The Okinawa issue remained a thorn in Washington's side, but it was no longer linked to a broader campaign to distance Japan from the United States. Although frustrations continued over our inability to get to closure, it was now a discrete, isolated issue, not linked to risks of weakening of the alliance.

In April 2010 Hatoyama was seated next to Obama at a dinner at the Nuclear Security Summit in Washington (our people positioned him there to give him an opportunity to speak with the president, though we did not want a bilateral meeting that would end in failure, as we knew it would at that time). Hatoyama began describing the difficult political position in which he found himself over Okinawa. Obama interrupted and said: "Let's cut to the chase. You said 'trust me' last November, meaning trust me to work this out. I am trusting you to do so. It hasn't happened yet. It must happen soon." Essentially accurate accounts of the conversation leaked to the Japanese press, from Japanese sources presumably hostile to Hatoyama. This further tightened the political noose around his neck.[6]

The North Koreans inadvertently helped move the issue in the right direction. In March a North Korean submarine sank the South Korean naval frigate *Cheonan*. South Korea's president, Lee Myung-bak, pressed Japan hard for support against North Korea. China seemed to be aligning itself with North Korea, or at a minimum indulging its unacceptable behavior. In April ten Chinese navy ships passed through waters just south of Okinawa in a maneuver that gained considerable attention in the Japanese media. These events were reminding the Japanese public of the country's difficult geostrategic position and the importance of its alliance with the United States. Having a prime minister out of step with that sentiment was a luxury that many Japanese judged they could ill afford.

Hatoyama read the writing on the wall. In late May he announced that his attempts to find an alternative to the Futenma Relocation plan had failed, and that Japan had to proceed with the original plan with minor modifications. He muddied this strategically correct decision by a rambling speech indicating he felt defeated and looked forward to the day when Japan could have a truly independent foreign policy. With that, he resigned. He was succeeded by Naoto Kan, who immediately began to distance himself from the dalliances with neutralism that had undermined Hatoyama and to make clear that the alliance with the United States was the centerpiece of his cabinet's foreign policy.

There were some suggestions that the U.S. administration had somehow engineered Hatoyama's downfall, which was manifestly not the case.[7] Hatoyama had undermined himself by pretending he had a mandate to reshape the alliance, whereas polls showed that in fact 80 percent of Japan's public supported the relationship. Hatoyama's fumbling badly damaged his standing with his own public. Washington's senior officials avoided giving public offense, or confronting him publicly, emphasizing the positive in the relationship. To do otherwise might have allowed Hatoyama to rally support for a policy of resisting American bullying. But we took a firm line on each of the points of departure Hatoyama proposed: Okinawa, the East Asia Community, and rebalancing of Japan's foreign policy. The Japanese public sided with the U.S. position. Hatoyama's inability to manage the U.S.-Japan alliance, combined with domestic failures, doomed his cabinet, which fell in May 2010.

While it unquestionably had been a rough ride from August 2009 to May 2010, our team felt considerable satisfaction with the outcome, and with the state of relations under Naoto Kan. Thanks to the support of the Japanese public and Kan's shift, we now had living proof that both major political parties in Japan, on the right and the left, could be relied upon to maintain and support the alliance and thus provide it with a more secure foundation. We believed that our patient but firm stewardship through a difficult period helped ensure that outcome.

SIX

CHINA:
THE OBAMA VISIT AND THE
CLIMATE CHANGE CONFERENCE

HAVING COMMITTED TO a November 2009 presidential visit to China, our national security team needed to lay the groundwork by identifying and making progress on the issues we expected to dominate the visit, principally Iran, North Korea, and climate change. But first, we had to deal with a politically sensitive issue that threatened to overshadow the visit—the Dalai Lama's plan to visit the United States in October.

KARMA PROBLEMS

The Dalai Lama's representatives had told us early in 2009 of his intention to do a multi-city tour of the United States, including a stop in Washington, in October. They expected the president to meet with him, as presidents have done periodically since George H. W. Bush.

China's leaders were extraordinarily sensitive about potential presidential meetings with the Dalai Lama, whom they described as a "secessionist" seeking Tibetan independence, so a meeting on the eve of Obama's trip to China was a lightning rod for them. Yet it was important for the president to make clear his intention to meet with the Dalai Lama to demonstrate U.S. support for his leadership, the religious and cultural aspirations of the Tibetan people, and his eventual return to Tibet.

Tibet had been occupied by the People's Liberation Army in 1950, with little serious challenge to China's rule there in the ensuing years. The

United States briefly flirted with the idea of self-determination for Tibet in the wake of the Dalai Lama's flight in 1959, and the Central Intelligence Agency (CIA) provided assistance to Tibetan liberation fighters in the late 1950s and for some time subsequently. With the U.S.-China rapprochement in the 1970s, however, U.S. expressions of concern about Tibet focused on the preservation of the unique cultural and religious traditions of the Tibetan people, not sovereignty or political status. These concerns were given added weight by the atrocities the Red Guards committed in Tibet during the Cultural Revolution, against both its people and its Buddhist monasteries and icons.

Since then, China's policy toward Tibet has varied periodically in significant respects, at times emphasizing the role of Tibetan ethnic officials, at other times the importance of economic development, but at all times the unshakable status of Tibet as part of China. In its implementation, this policy has consistently repressed Buddhist monks and others loyal to the Dalai Lama and the pre-1959 regime, demonized the Dalai Lama as a proponent of independence for Tibet, and rejected outside interference, by the United States, India, or anyone else.[1] China's rule has been marked by periods of unrest, demonstrations, and riots, most recently in 2008, but by no serious challenge to its control.

Over the first few months of the Obama administration, the Chinese informed our officials of their "core concerns," namely, their claimed sovereignty over Taiwan and Tibet. They warned privately that a presidential meeting with the Dalai Lama shortly before the president's visit to Beijing would have grave, unspecified consequences for the U.S.-China relationship and for the visit. I responded each time that it was critical for Beijing to resume its dialogue with the Dalai Lama, which had begun in the 1980s and was resumed in 2002 after a decade and a half of suspension.

I have long had a close relationship with the Dalai Lama and with his Washington representative, Lodi Gyari, who has served as the Dalai Lama's personal representative in the dialogue with Beijing. Gyari knew of my sympathy for the Dalai Lama and the religious and cultural aspirations of Tibetans, and we had communicated freely and candidly with each other for years, despite our different perspectives on China.

I thought I might be able to persuade Gyari to consider rescheduling the Dalai Lama's visit to Washington until after the president's visit to China. Although I believed the meeting to be important, I thought there was nothing magical about the October date. A meeting after, rather than before, Obama's trip to China would convey the same level of support, but without the collateral damage to the U.S.-China relationship and the president's trip. A later meeting, in my view, would open the possibility of restoring dialogue between Beijing and the Dalai Lama, which I knew Gyari favored. Ultimately, any progress or solution would have to emerge from discussions between Beijing and the Dalai Lama, and I did not want to arrange a sequence of meetings that would set back both U.S.-China relations and the prospect of a Chinese-Tibetan dialogue. So I broached the subject of delay with Gyari.

Gyari was distressed at the suggestion that the meeting be moved. The Dalai Lama's visit to the United States enco.npassed five cities, he pointed out, and could not be changed. Large security deposits had already been made to reserve concert halls and auditoriums around the country for his teaching sessions, which typically drew 15,000–20,000 devotees. I told Gyari I had no instructions to seek a change in the date and indeed had deliberately not raised the issue with the president. The president had genuine and profound respect for the Dalai Lama, I told him, and they would indeed meet. But I asked him to explore whether a date after November might work, and whether the Dalai Lama might so decide on his own, not at our request. Gyari agreed to explore it.

Gyari returned to the Tibetan capital in exile in Dharamsala, in northern India, and talked over the situation with the Dalai Lama. The spiritual leader understood U.S. concerns and suggested that he might be able to come two months earlier instead, in August, and then proceed with his visit to other American cities in October. I thought this was a plausible compromise that would elicit an acceptable response from the Chinese. At the same time, the arrangement would not look as if the administration was rebuffing the Dalai Lama and thus draw criticism that could undercut domestic political support for our China policy and make it much more difficult to implement.

Other senior officials at the State Department and the National Security Council disagreed, arguing the proposal still risked a strong reaction from the Chinese that would shake the foundations we were trying to build. In fact, throughout 2009 the Chinese had consistently singled out this issue as the one posing the greatest immediate threat to the relationship. Accordingly, I conveyed to Gyari that August would not work.

Gyari took one last run at me in July, in a meeting in my office joined by ambassador-designate to Beijing Jon Huntsman. Our position did not change.

To compensate for delaying the date of the Dalai Lama's visit, we decided to send the assistant to the president for intergovernmental affairs, Valerie Jarrett, to Dharamsala in September. Jarrett was the highest executive branch official ever to visit Dharamsala. Given her exceptionally close relationship with the president, dating back to the early 1990s in Chicago, she was able to convey convincingly his personal commitment to the Dalai Lama. As we had agreed upon before Jarrett's visit, the Dalai Lama announced the following day that he had personally decided not to seek a meeting with the president in October.[2]

While our people were preparing for Jarrett's visit to Dharamsala, we sought assurances the Chinese would resume dialogue with the Dalai Lama. The Chinese refused to make an explicit commitment, but sent unmistakable signals they would meet with the Dalai Lama's representative after Obama's visit to China.

In October, around the time of the Dalai Lama's visit to other cities in the United States, his Washington-based supporters leaked a tendentious version of this history to the *Washington Post*. The published account failed to note that the president intended to meet with the Dalai Lama after Obama's November trip to China and the implicit quid pro quo of a resumed dialogue between the Dalai Lama and Beijing (neither of which the journalist knew about). Quoting an American scholar on Tibet, Robert Barnett, the article charged, "We've got the classic case of a Western government yet again conceding to Chinese pressure that is imaginary long after that Chinese pressure has ceased to exist. The Chinese must be falling over themselves with astonishment at what Western diplomats will give them without being asked. I don't know what the poker analogy would be. 'Please, see all my cards and take my money, too'?" (Ironically, we had received word from this same scholar some months earlier urging us *not* to meet with the Dalai Lama in October.) The report left the impression that the administration had decided to turn its back on the Dalai Lama in order to appease China, whereas the delay by a few months was actually calculated to benefit both the Tibetans and U.S.-China equities.[3]

The damage to the public perception of the administration's China policy was considerable. Editorialists and op-ed writers piled on.[4] None ever entertained the notion that a meeting with the Dalai Lama in early 2010 would be a sign of respect comparable to a meeting in October 2009. No one wrote of the potential benefits of fostering a favorable atmosphere for a resumed Beijing–Dalai Lama dialogue, instead of dooming it to a long respite by insisting on a presidential meeting with the Dalai Lama in October. The importance of building a strong foundation for the U.S.-China relationship early in the term was written off as cynical or naïve, or both. Rather, the implicit assumption seemed to be that unless the Chinese were confronted and offended, the meeting with the Dalai Lama was barely worth having.

Editorialists and human rights activists now could point to two events to support allegations that the Obama administration was prepared to, as some liked to say, "kowtow" to the Chinese on human rights issues: Secretary Clinton's remark about U.S. willingness to cooperate on global issues even while trading talking points on human rights and Taiwan, and the fracas over the Dalai Lama meeting. The way in which these two incidents were conflated and elevated into something resembling administration doctrine illustrates the difficulty of conducting a serious foreign policy in a public domain dominated by superficial discourse, in which sound bites substitute for a sound assessment of the costs and benefits of different approaches.

FIRST DISCUSSIONS ON IRAN

Throughout 2009 our foreign policy team was also working to gain Chinese support for our approach on critical global issues, which we saw as our highest priority in the relationship. In the spring we had succeeded in gaining Chinese support for UN Security Council action condemning North Korea's ballistic missile and nuclear tests, which imposed real costs on Pyongyang. The UN Security Council Resolution called for a near-total embargo on arms exports and imports and sanctions on financial institutions doing business with North Korea.

By fall, the administration's principal concern was Iran's nuclear program. Teheran had failed to respond to Obama's offer in the first half of 2009 to open a dialogue. All the while, Iran was pursuing its uranium enrichment program in defiance of UN Security Council resolutions. Its secret facility in Qom was already known to U.S. intelligence. Obama decided that if the negotiating track with Iran was to have any chance of success, the pressure track had to be strengthened. That required the help of China, not only as a permanent member of the UN Security Council but also as Iran's largest trading partner and a major investor in Iran's energy sector, as noted earlier.

When President Obama met with President Hu at the UN General Assembly in September, Iran was the principal topic of discussion. Stressing the unacceptability of Iran's program, the president called on all five permanent members of the UN Security Council, which included China, to send an unequivocal message to Teheran. He was willing to negotiate in good faith to terminate and dismantle Iran's nuclear weapons program, he said, but a credible "pressure track" was also needed to persuade Iran to respond. In reply, Hu urged the United States to talk directly with Iran and to show greater flexibility. Obama returned to the subject repeatedly, making clear to Hu that it was the defining security issue in the U.S.-China relationship at that time.[5]

In the wake of the president's September 2009 meeting with Hu, his top advisers decided to drive the point home by instructing Dennis Ross and me to undertake a special mission to China focusing exclusively on Iran. Ross was the NSC's senior director for the Central Region, which covered a vast swath of countries stretching from Morocco to India, and he was the administration's lead strategist on Iran. Having worked on Middle East issues for three administrations of both parties, Ross enjoyed unique international respect and credibility. It was judged that through such a special mission he and I could effectively convey to the Chinese the urgent need for action against Iran.[6]

We met with State Councilor Dai Bingguo, Foreign Minister Yang Jiechi, and other senior officials. Ross's message was forceful and direct. Time, he said, was not our ally. The nations of the world now faced three ticking clocks. The first was the Iranian nuclear program, which was proceeding toward high enrichment of uranium. The second was the Israeli clock. The Israelis, Ross made clear, would not accept a nuclear-armed Iran. They would take strong action against what they saw as an existential threat. The ability of China and the United States to dissuade them should not be overestimated. The third was the Saudi clock. The Saudis viewed Iran with barely less alarm than Israel did and the United States was convinced they would not passively accept an Iranian nuclear weapons program.

Israel
US would not accept a nuclear armed Iran neither would
Saudi Arabia

As was commonly the case, the Chinese showed no immediate sign of being persuaded by our arguments. But Ross and I came away confident that our message had been heard, and that we would see greater Chinese cooperation on Iran in the future.

OBAMA VISITS CHINA: REALITY VERSUS MESSAGING

In November 2009 Obama embarked on his first trip to Asia as president, visiting in succession Japan, Singapore, China, and South Korea. The trip's itinerary was structured to demonstrate not only the administration's desire to build relations with China during Obama's first year in office, but also to put it in the context of U.S. relations with allies and key security partners.

Planning for the trip focused on several objectives, the first being to decide on the right messages for Obama's meetings with Hu Jintao and other Chinese leaders. The resulting agenda emphasized Iran's nuclear program, North Korea, economic issues (including, in particular, the undervaluation of China's currency), the need for progress at the climate change conference the following month in Copenhagen, Sudan and the genocide in Darfur, human rights, and Tibet.

In his meeting with Hu, the president placed these issues in a broader context of desired cooperation between the United States and China. He laid out his global priorities and argued that confrontation would serve none of them, while cooperation would advance all of them. He also rebutted directly the common Chinese belief that the United States sought to contain China or restrain its growth.

As usual, the subjects that produced the sharpest disagreement were human rights, Tibet, and Taiwan. On human rights, Hu indicated no intention to respond to U.S. concerns about political prisoners. On Tibet, Hu asked the president to decline all future meetings with the Dalai Lama. Obama replied coolly that he intended to meet the Dalai Lama in the future in the Dalai Lama's capacity as a representative of the religious and cultural aspirations of Tibetans. On Taiwan, Hu called on the United States to halt the sale of all arms, particularly sophisticated weapons, to Taiwan. Obama replied that U.S. arms sales would be consistent with the three U.S.-China Joint Communiqués, and he added in their subsequent joint press conference that U.S. conduct would also accord with the Taiwan Relations Act, which mandated such sales.

Otherwise, the private talks generally emphasized the positive, with Hu repeatedly stressing China's commitment to a cooperative relationship with the United States. On Iran, Obama continued the drumbeat he had begun in their meeting in September, stressing the need for pressure to change Iran's calculations about the desirability of developing nuclear weapons. Hu again called for a direct U.S.-Iran dialogue but emphatically rejected Iran's nuclear weapons pretensions.

China's economic challenges were the subject of a lively discussion at a lunch hosted by Premier Wen Jiabao, during which the president and Larry Summers tried to persuade Wen that a properly valued currency would help them address their economic problems, while Wen talked about the difficulties of managing an economy with the scale of poverty still afflicting China.

The second objective of the trip was to issue a joint statement, which the two sides painfully negotiated. I was frankly unenthusiastic about the prospect of a joint statement, not only because I was designated to be the principal negotiator of the document but also because joint statements have an unhappy history in U.S.-China relations; only the Nixon/Kissinger Shanghai Communiqué received public acclaim while the others were picked apart by critics. My feeling was that no one paid any attention to the good language in these statements, whereas everyone was ready to leap on anything perceived as a concession—as if such documents could be negotiated without concessions. But there was a consensus on the U.S. side that a realistic statement of the cooperative aspects of our relationship was an important message for audiences in the United States, China, and overseas, and we proceeded.

So I spent tens of hours negotiating and leading a negotiating team with Chinese counterparts that ultimately produced a forty-one-paragraph document issued during the president's visit. The final document was, I thought, a good compendium of our joint objectives. It contained new and unusual language in which the Chinese "welcome[d] the United States as an Asia-Pacific nation that contributes to peace, stability and prosperity in the region," noteworthy and desirable because of suspicions that China planned to seek the ultimate expulsion of the United States from the region. It stressed that promoting human rights and democracy is an important part of U.S. policy. It called for a resumption of U.S.-China military-to-military exchanges, suspended by the Chinese since President George W. Bush's congressional notification of arms sales to

Taiwan in October 2008. We reiterated traditional language on Taiwan, resisting Chinese attempts to strengthen it. The document highlighted the importance of terminating the nuclear weapons programs of Iran and North Korea. It also laid out an agenda for cooperation on clean energy development and a successful outcome in the Copenhagen climate change conference the following month.

The joint statement was by and large welcomed by Asia experts, who saw it as a signal that the United States and China could work together on a broad agenda of issues. The former U.S. ambassador to Thailand, Mort Abramowitz, one of the "wise men" of U.S. Asia policy, wrote an article praising it as an unusually comprehensive and detailed program for common action.[7]

Criticism came from two sources, one expected and one unexpected. Some in Taiwan were uneasy when they heard "the two countries reiterated that the fundamental principle of respect for each other's sovereignty and territorial integrity is at the core of the three U.S.-China joint communiqués which guide U.S.-China relations. The two sides agreed that respecting each other's core interests is extremely important to ensure steady progress in U.S.-China relations." The Chinese had pushed up to the last minute for language specifying that opposition to the independence of Tibet and Xinjiang was in China's "core interests," which we refused. We also made clear that U.S. policy toward Taiwan was not subject to alteration through this document. Criticism of the joint statement in Taiwan was muted by the government's awareness that the language conveyed no new changes and reiterated long-standing policy. Indeed, Assistant Secretary of State Kurt Campbell and I had coordinated extensively with Taiwan officials in negotiating the document, which occasioned one frustrated outburst by our Chinese negotiating partner, the very intelligent and capable Vice Foreign Minister He Yafei, about what he called a "three-way negotiation," between the U.S., the People's Republic of China, and Taiwan.

More surprising was the reaction of the Indian press, which sharply criticized two sentences that "welcomed all efforts conducive to peace, stability, and development in South Asia . . . and support[ed] the improvement and growth of relations between India and Pakistan." It was hard for me to conceive of two more anodyne sentences, and candidly none of us gave a second thought to including them in the document. The hostile

Indian domestic reaction caused enough of a stir for Prime Minister Man-mohan Singh to object to the language when he met with President Obama in Washington a week later. I realized in retrospect that the spe-cific language was beside the point. The episode was a reminder of Indian resentment of hints of the U.S. mediating in its relations with Pakistan, and how hypersensitive India is about any suggestion that China has a legitimate role in any aspect of South Asian security because of Indian anxieties over China and its close relationship with Pakistan.[8]

The third concern was the messaging conveyed during the president's public appearances and in his speeches. This proved to be the most con-troversial aspect of the trip.

The centerpiece of the president's public appearances was a town hall event that he presided over in Shanghai. In place of the usual presidential speech, it was decided that a town hall meeting resembling a campaign appearance would send a stronger message to Chinese audiences of how democracies functioned. The downside of the format, of course, was that it made Chinese officialdom nervous. They do not have town hall meet-ings. So once the idea was proposed by our side and reluctantly accepted by the Chinese, every detail of its organization was the subject of intense and painful hand-to-hand combat. The Chinese were particularly uneasy because the event would take place the day before Obama's meetings with Hu, which they considered the high point of the visit, and saw it as a venue in which Obama might broadcast unwelcome messages or criti-cisms, especially on human rights.

Our people wanted an audience of 1,500. The Chinese insisted that the numbers be restricted to 500. We wanted the event to be streamed live on a Chinese news website. The Chinese insisted that there be no video streaming. We wanted it to be broadcast on Chinese Central Television (CCTV). The answer was no. We wanted to ensure that the attendees were not handpicked by the Communist Party. The Chinese resisted our effort to open up the event to a broad audience. We wanted no Chinese moderator. They wanted one.

I called in the Chinese chargé d'affaires to warn him that their obstruc-tionism threatened the success of the president's visit, pointing out that we would not seek to control an event of this kind organized by President Hu in the United States. He replied that the Foreign Ministry would do what it could to accommodate our requests, but it should be seen as a joint event sensitive to the customs of the host. I warned that we might pull the plug on the whole event, with accompanying embarrassment to all.

However, we decided to go ahead because we had achieved our bottom line, though not our ideal. The transcript of President Obama's opening remarks and answers to questions was streamed live on a Chinese news website, Xinhua.net, without censorship in the first showing (though it was censored subsequently). While not shown on CCTV, it was broadcast live on Shanghai TV, with a potential audience of up to 200 million. We were able to invite some guests, and our understanding was that the other guests were almost all students, not party functionaries, invited by deans and faculties of the universities. There was no Chinese moderator, as President Obama interacted directly with the Chinese students.

For those of our team who attended, the event seemed to go very well. President Obama was greeted with warm applause. The students listened with rapt attention throughout, and they had the same obvious respect, rapport, and regard for Obama that I have become accustomed to seeing in audiences throughout the world. Questioners were transparently thrilled by the opportunity to ask questions of a world leader, not a common occurrence in their own country, and laughter and giggles accompanied numerous answers.

The first half of the president's opening remarks covered the importance of U.S.-China relations, then provided a lengthy tribute to the U.S. system of democracy, freedom, protection of human rights, and constitutional law.[9] It was meant to provide to an audience living under a different system a vision of what we saw as a politically just system and to discreetly promote self-examination on their part. In fact, the remarks were modeled on a superb and well-received speech by President Ronald Reagan at Fudan University in 1984 that followed the same format and contained similar themes.[10]

We subsequently learned that in the first twenty-four hours of Xinhua.net streaming the president's remarks received 55 million hits by Chinese viewers (we also streamed them live on the White House website in the event of problems in China, and that produced additional viewers). An event that exposed scores of millions of Chinese to themes of democracy and human rights on the Internet and television seemed well worth the aggravations.

But that was not how the U.S. press chose to cover the event. Led by a front-page story in the *New York Times*, journalists dug deeply into all the steps the Chinese had undertaken to try to constrain the event.[11] They left the impression of a president who accepted Chinese censorship, pulled his punches, and participated in a Potemkin village event not seen by real Chinese. These themes were parroted by other papers and editorialists, fitting as they did a broader narrative that the media had been advertising in the run-up to the visit—namely, China was a rising power, the United States a declining power, it owed them $1 trillion, and it came as a supplicant. An inaccurate and distorted account of the town hall provided all the evidence that was needed to confirm the preview.

The absurdity of the account did little to diminish its popularity. Our delegation was not in a position to impose our conditions on an event hosted by China, of course, except to make it conform to our general objectives, which we did. China is not England. That is precisely why we decided on a town hall event, well aware of the problems. We knew perfectly well going in that the Communist Party would do what it could to constrain the audience. To reach a large Chinese audience, which we did despite Chinese efforts, was after all the point of the event, to show that a message on democracy and human rights can get through in the face of resistance.

The Chinese imposed constraints on two other public events, both of which fed the U.S. media account of the U.S. as a supplicant. First, Press Secretary Robert Gibbs and I discovered only three hours before the joint press conference that there would be no questions, only statements by the two presidents. Our press advance team had unwisely accepted the Chinese standard practice of refusing questions without raising it to political levels for challenge. Second, we decided that the president would give his only interview in China to a cutting-edge, unorthodox newspaper called *Southern Weekend*, which often published critical pieces that no other Chinese paper would run. Before the interview, the Communist Party's Publicity and Information Department (formerly named the Propaganda Department) called in the *Southern Weekend*'s journalists and instructed them not to ask the tougher questions they had prepared. They also engaged in a clumsy attempt to censor the end product, unaccountably ripping out the interview pages of the newspaper that went to expatriates in China while failing to censor other hard copies and websites.[12]

For those of us accustomed to dealing with the Chinese censorship system, none of these developments was surprising. Our objective in organizing these events was not to tear down the Chinese system of censorship nor to accommodate it, but to penetrate it. We succeeded in large measure. But in terms of American public perceptions of the trip, the Western media coverage of these events damaged both the trip and the administration's ability to manage China policy.

The president was deeply frustrated by that coverage. I discussed it with him on Air Force One subsequently. As usual, he spoke analytically and with equanimity, not as a victim. But his perception that we were faced with discussions of public policy that were based more on myth than reality, on a preference for the sensationalist over the important, on a preference for attack rather than balance, was apparent. The frustration over the China stop was aggravated by the story about the first stop, also in the *New York Times* and discussed earlier, asserting that Obama had abandoned Secretary Robert Gates's policy on U.S. basing rights in Okinawa—which was the exact opposite of what the president had done and happily was understood by the Japanese press covering the visit.

I drew several conclusions from the trip. One was that the administration was managing the key issues in the U.S.-China relationship reasonably well, making progress on some, such as Iran, climate change, North Korea, and economic problems. The trip had also achieved a familiarity and degree of comfort between the two nations' leaders that would serve as a safety net if and when serious problems arose. By being properly embedded in a larger regional tour, the China visit undercut concerns in the region that the United States might accommodate China to the exclusion of their interests. The president had performed in his characteristically commanding fashion in the meetings with Hu and Wen and thereby, in my view, erased doubts they may have harbored about whether this previously unknown figure was ready for the world stage. The Chinese leaders conveyed clearly their desire for a cooperative, not a confrontational, relationship with the United States.

But I also concluded that the administration, and I, had to do a much better job of getting our public message out to key U.S. media outlets. When an attractive but false narrative takes hold, it is very difficult to shake it, and that is what happened with the "U.S. as supplicant" story. For the remainder of my time in the administration, I would make much greater efforts to get across our point of view, particularly our aggressive pursuit of U.S. interests, to the best journalists before rather than after a problem arose; I would try to ensure that the more balanced and sophisticated journalists knew what we were doing and could write with knowledge. In the run-up to subsequent major events, in particular Hu Jintao's visit to the United States in January 2011, we made sure that the public messaging part of the visit received proportionately much greater attention and was thought through more carefully.

I took away small lessons as well. When the Chinese first saw me about Hu's 2011 visit, I made it clear that there would be questions at the press conference. They came back at me three or four times subsequently, deploying a variety of curious arguments, such as we could save forty minutes and have lunch closer to the scheduled time if we eliminated any Q&A. We did not budge. I also resolved never again to sacrifice the tens of hours negotiating a joint statement that diverted me from the other preparatory aspects of a visit, especially the public messaging. In January 2011 we relied on a much more coordinated team effort, and the State Department's assistant secretary for East Asia and Pacific affairs, Kurt Campbell, led the team that negotiated the joint statement, doing an excellent job and freeing me to concentrate on the White House's strategic objectives.

COPENHAGEN: SNATCHING VICTORY, OR SOMETHING LIKE IT, FROM THE JAWS OF DEFEAT

The Obama administration placed great importance on addressing the challenge of climate change, which it judged had been given short shrift by the Bush administration. In addition to seeking cap-and-trade legislation domestically, a goal that was not achieved, Obama sought to negotiate an international understanding that would impose obligations of comparable standing on all countries.[13] At some point during his first year in office, China passed the United States as the leading emitter of greenhouse gases in the world, driven by its explosive growth and energy consumption. However, the United States and Europe were still responsible for the overwhelming majority of so-called legacy emissions (those greenhouse gases emitted earlier and still in the earth's atmosphere). President Obama felt that as a matter of justice and political necessity, an international agreement on climate change could not be reached unless China undertook serious commitments. He knew it was unrealistic, and unfair, to expect China, as a country with less than 10 percent of America's per capita gross domestic product (GDP), to be subject to commitments of the same scale as those required of the United States and Europe. But in his view they needed to have the same enforceability and validity under international law, both because it was indefensible for the world's largest emitter to be exempt from international obligations and because Congress would use such an exemption to block cap-and-trade legislation.

The president raised the need for a constructive Chinese position on climate change in each of his meetings with Hu. By the late fall of 2009, it was apparent that the Chinese position was not evolving much, and agreement at the international conference scheduled for December in Copenhagen would be impossible without some change. So a more intensive effort was made to alter China's position. The president wrote a private letter to Hu on the subject. The United States refined its position, making clear what was most needed from the Chinese: a substantial commitment to slow its production of greenhouse gases, a mechanism to verify each country's compliance with its commitments, and an understanding that all commitments, including China's and America's, were equally binding.

By late November, negotiations between the State Department and the Chinese seemed to be stalled, even degenerating occasionally into public shouting matches. On the U.S. side, the deputy director of the National Economic Council, Mike Froman, became more deeply engaged, always a helpful development given Froman's substantial capabilities, his closeness to the president, and his problem-solving approach to issues. The Chinese came forward in November with a satisfactory offer on the production of greenhouse gases, pledging to reduce carbon intensity (that is, CO_2 emissions per unit of GDP output) by 40–45 percent from current levels by 2020. But they showed no movement on verification or the legally binding character of all commitments.

President Obama decided to attend the December 16–18 heads-of-state conference in Copenhagen. He was under pressure from other world leaders, most of whom planned to attend, and from NGOs, and he did not want to see the United States singled out as the cause of the conference's failure. Through a phone call and correspondence in the preceding month, he had sought to persuade President Hu that the United States and China ran the risk of being blamed collectively for failure, noting that Americans did not accept the European demand for draconian reductions and were more realistic.

The president arrived in Copenhagen in the early morning of December 18 for what was intended to be a one-day marathon of negotiations and meetings. Upon arrival, we learned that negotiations had made no last-minute progress on key issues, which remained by and large unresolved. Conferences involving heads of state, no less participants from 100 countries or more, are not well designed for resolving problems. This one was distinctly not, with mediocre chairmanship by the Danish prime minister, profound divisions among numerous blocs of competing interests, and showboating by provocateurs like Hugo Chávez of Venezuela.

Secretary Clinton summed it up to our delegation privately. After witnessing several hours of histrionics, she commented with a smile that she was haunted by the image of a meteor heading toward earth, bringing imminent destruction, and the likely reactions of this collection of world leaders. The poorer developing countries would demand reparations. The larger developing countries would egg them on. Numerous countries would blame the United States. Committees would be formed, speeches would be made, and agendas would be promulgated. But almost no one would discuss what to do about the problem.

The Chinese delegation had been unhelpful, at times ornery and even destructive, pitting developing countries against developed countries, insisting that high levels of "reparations" for legacy emissions be provided to developing countries, and digging in its heels on both verification and the legal character of agreements. The president met with the head of the Chinese delegation, Premier Wen Jiabao, with whom he had a good relationship since their candid discussion about economic issues at a friendly lunch in Beijing a month earlier. They met for an hour and had what seemed like a productive exchange. While neither gave away substantive ground, Wen agreed that our two sets of negotiators should meet and that the president and premier should reconvene later in the day.

The American and Chinese negotiators met and got nowhere. In the meantime, the twenty key delegations met in plenary session to see if problems could be resolved. Wen did not attend the session, sending instead a vice minister far down the pecking order to deal with President

Obama, Angela Merkel, Nicolas Sarkozy, Gordon Brown, Kevin Rudd, and others. When the vice minister attempted to rebut a statement by the president on the character and adequacy of the trust fund for developing countries being set up by the developed countries, Obama said that he saw no point in continuing discussions unless delegations like China's included people at the political level who could make decisions, not arguments.

We were planning to leave Copenhagen on Air Force One between 6 and 7 p.m. The urgency of keeping close to our schedule was heightened by reports that Washington was on the brink of the largest snowstorm in its history, which would make it impossible to land if we delayed. The president called me in to ask my view on why the Chinese were so dug in. Beyond noting the difficulty of the substance, I said the Chinese are traditionally not the most nimble negotiators in international conferences because they have to obtain the consensus of the leadership. Since Wen was one of nine members of the Politburo Standing Committee, it was very difficult for him to move. The president asked if I thought another meeting was worth it, whether there might be any further Chinese flexibility. I said I thought it best in any event to try once more at a minimum, so that we would not be blamed for any failure. He asked me to call the Chinese delegation to arrange a meeting with Premier Wen to give it one last shot. Which I did.

The Chinese delegation told me they would check with the premier but did not respond for an hour and a half. During that time, we learned that most of the delegation, including Wen, had gone to the airport, expecting to leave without an agreement. Apparently after hearing of Obama's suggestion to meet again, Wen returned to the convention center. The Chinese finally consented to meet at 6 p.m., then pushed it back to 7 p.m. In the meantime, we reached out to South Africa's president Jacob Zuma and India's prime minister Singh to see if they wished to meet. In the process we learned that they were meeting with Wen Jiabao. The president told us he might as well head up to the Wen meeting at 7 p.m., expecting to join the Indians, South Africans, and Brazilians, who had all been closely coordinating positions for several months. He concluded that the best way to reach a deal was to see them all at once. We did not, however, inform the Chinese that we hoped to join their group meeting, only that we would be there at 7 p.m.

I went up to the hallway outside the conference room where the president was to meet with Wen at 7 p.m. The hall was lined with a gaggle of Chinese security agents, journalists, protocol officers, and other hangers-on. Secretary Clinton arrived a minute later. An officious Chinese protocol officer tried to guide us down the hall in the opposite direction to a waiting room at some distance from the China, Brazil, India, and South Africa meeting. As he headed down the hall, Secretary Clinton said to me, "No, we're not going there. We'll wait here," at the top of the stairs. At that moment President Obama appeared, bounding up the stairs along with his close aide Denis McDonough. I assumed that Secret Service people were accompanying him, but not visibly so.

Secretary Clinton and I quickly huddled with him and pointed him toward the conference room where Wen was meeting with counterparts. The president started down the narrow hallway, with startled Chinese security, protocol, and others parting like the Red Sea for Moses. The Chinese protocol officer who had attempted to steer Secretary Clinton and me to a distant conference room came running up to us from behind, attempting to divert us. I blocked him with my not very bulky body. We continued down the hall, shouting, "The president is coming through." We arrived at the closed door to the meeting, blocked by a phalanx of bystanders. The president eased his way in, helped at this point by the Secret Service. Secretary Clinton and I were on his heels, and had to burst, shoulders down, through the phalanx as in a goal-line plunge.

We landed in the room to see a startled group of heads of government—a smiling but clearly surprised Wen Jiabao, Prime Minister Singh, President Lula of Brazil, and President Zuma. Obama greeted the group, exclaiming, "Premier Wen, great to see you!" He then said, "I'd like to sit next to my friend Lula," who was sitting opposite Wen, and we found our way in.

I stood over on the side next to a smiling Denis McDonough, who whispered to me, "These guys don't know what they're in for. They've never encountered anyone like Barack Obama before."

Obama proceeded to crisply lay out what was needed for a deal. He described the agreements on the trust fund for developing countries, and on obtaining acceptable emission reduction commitments from the major players. He said what we needed now was agreement on a nonintrusive verification mechanism to ensure that countries were doing what they pledged, on the comparable legal character of all commitments whether by Kyoto Protocol signatories or not, and on language sought by the European Union aiming at a legally binding agreement. He proposed specific language designed to address the verification issue.

Lula followed Obama's presentation with an outburst about the arrogance of the West and its demands. Obama replied curtly, "I've come here accepting most of what you've decided. I've made a modest proposal. You don't want to talk about it? Fine. I have plenty to do in Washington. Plus we have a historic snowstorm coming in. I'm happy to leave." Wen, who was running the meeting for the non-Americans, urged Obama to stay and Lula to be patient.

A wrangle ensued for an hour and a half, in English, Chinese, and Portuguese. After Obama's sharp retort to Lula, none of the other heads of government appeared anxious to engage in a dispute with Obama. For the most part, they left it to their environment ministers to argue against the language Obama was proposing. One of the senior Chinese negotiators, the very capable vice chairman of the powerful National Development and Reform Commission, Xie Zhenhua, red-faced with frustration, intervened at one point to loudly exclaim in Chinese that Obama was wrong about the comparable character of commitments by developed and developing countries. Wen instructed his interpreter not to translate the comments into English, saying (inaccurately) that he had already made that point. Rising to his feet, Xie later had an even stronger outburst. Again, Wen told the interpreter to remain silent, and signaled to Xie to remain in his seat. Obama smiled and said he did not fully catch the translation but he assumed Xie was expressing enthusiasm for the progress made so far. An evidently amused Wen smiled. India's environment minister, Jairam Ramesh, argued politely but aggressively with Obama over several points. Finally, Wen intervened, saying that he thought the last proposal by Obama addressed their concerns.

As Obama was about to leave, Wen asked him, astonishingly, if Obama could sell the agreement to the G-77. One would have thought the leading developing countries in the room might have undertaken that task, but Obama's performance seemed to persuade Wen that he was the man for the job. Obama replied that he first needed to speak to representatives from the European Union and developed countries to get their endorsement, but he would do what he could in his little remaining time.

President Obama then spoke to German Chancellor Angela Merkel, Canadian Prime Minister Stephen Harper, French President Nicolas Sarkozy, and UK Prime Minister Gordon Brown. They reluctantly assented, Obama having gotten more from the Chinese, Brazilians, Indians, and South Africans than they had but still short of their hoped-for agreement on a legally binding treaty. Our delegation then rushed to the airport, taking off three minutes before the drop-dead time to beat the peak of the snowstorm. We landed at Andrews Air Force Base with a foot of snow already on the ground and a blinding storm continuing. We left behind in Copenhagen a State Department and White House team that spent another couple of days of hard negotiations with developing countries before they finally accepted the outlines of what President Obama had worked out with the big four.

The significance of the achievement in terms of addressing the climate change challenge can be debated. It certainly was a better outcome than the complete breakdown that appeared imminent when President Obama arrived, and there can be little doubt that he played the indispensable role in stitching together an agreement. The president and others in the administration concluded that they did not want this process repeated, and the 2010 Cancun conference was left for lower-ranking officials from most countries. The dream of a legally binding agreement was effectively shelved for some time to come. At the same time, many of us believed that to seriously address climate change, encouraging technological fixes was orders of magnitude more effective than international conferences. But the president did pull together a basic framework that the major countries now all accept, with commitments on limiting emissions and a mechanism for verifying compliance with stated intentions.

As for U.S.-China relations, the events in and surrounding Copenhagen showed the necessity, the possibilities, and the limits of cooperation on climate change. Beijing's objectives were substantially different from Washington's. The Chinese would have wrecked the conference if left to their own devices. Thanks to Obama's cajoling, they, and Wen in particular, realized at the last minute that China would bear the lion's share of the blame if the conference collapsed. Accordingly, Wen worked with Obama at that final chaotic meeting to ensure success. The evaluation of Europeans was not so generous, as a spate of comments by their leaders and media blamed China for the shortcomings of the outcome. The Chinese seemed bewildered by these assessments, suggesting the dimensions of the time lag between the growing reality of China's international strength today and its own still limited perception of its responsibilities.

The meeting served to remind those of us in the administration who attended of Obama's unique strengths and qualities. He showed a determination to get a result under an impossible deadline. He gambled by bursting into the Chinese meeting with its friends, ignoring the risk of rebuff. With forceful eloquence and obvious mastery of the technical details as well as political stakes, he outargued four delegations, including heads of state and environmental experts. And he came out of the meeting to find the Chinese asking him to intervene with developing countries on behalf of the deal. There was no doubt in the minds of those of us who saw this spectacle play out that each of the leaders, including those from China, felt they were dealing with a formidable figure and had acquired a new and greater respect for the president. The Chinese also came to recognize the truth of his argument that the two nations needed to work together to avoid being blamed for failure. This helped boost U.S. credibility in addressing future issues with comparable gaps in objectives.[14]

SEVEN

YEAR TWO:
DEALING WITH AN ASSERTIVE CHINA

As 2010 BEGAN, we felt we had laid a good foundation for relations with China through a considered strategy. Our approach rested on three principles.

First, China should not be considered an inevitable adversary, but rather a potential partner in resolving critical global issues. The president understood there were competitive elements in its relationship with the United States—some quite significant—in both the economic and the security areas, but he believed the cooperative elements could and should outweigh those. Washington did not seek the containment of China, as was the case with the Soviet Union, both because of the inherent differences between those two nations and because of the hopelessness of pursuing such a policy toward a country that was much more profoundly integrated into the global system. Rather, the president welcomed a strong, prosperous, and successful China that would play a stronger leadership role on global issues.[1] The administration was prepared to recognize and accept China's legitimate interests and to show them the respect that its leaders and people craved. In keeping with this approach, the president met with Hu Jintao four times in his first year in office, called him on the phone several times, agreed to the establishment of a broad strategic and economic dialogue, and approved a joint statement stressing the emerging partnership.

Second, while welcoming China's rise, the administration believed it was essential that it occur within the context of international law and norms. That meant China should not resort to force or intimidation in resolving international disputes. It should conform to international economic norms and rules established in trade by the World Trade Organization (WTO); on currency by the International Monetary Fund (IMF); and on aid, export credit finance, and overseas investment by the Organization for Economic Cooperation and Development (OECD) and the world's major economic and assistance actors. Furthermore, the U.S.-China economic relationship had to be mutually beneficial, and the trade imbalance and market access problems needed to be addressed in conformity with IMF and WTO standards and U.S. economic interests. China should accept the principles of freedom of navigation established by the Law of the Sea Convention, defining the rights and responsibilities of nations in their use of the world's oceans. It was critical for China to work with the other five permanent members of the UN Security Council to halt the proliferation of nuclear weapons, particularly in North Korea and Iran. China should accept responsibility for curtailing climate change. We would continue to urge China to conform to universal standards on human rights.

Third, the administration sought to ensure that China's rise served to stabilize, not destabilize, the Asia-Pacific region, which included five U.S. allies and other partners in whose security Americans had an interest. These countries shared a common perspective: none of them wanted to see the United States and China in a conflict or rivalry that forced them to choose sides. At the same time, many, arguably all, felt uneasy about the consequences of China's rise and what it might mean for their own security and other interests. They believed that a strong U.S. presence—political, economic, and forward-deployed military—was critical to ensure that they did not fall under the exclusive sway of a dominant new power in the region with which they all had substantial historical experience, for better or worse. Our foreign policy team saw three principal ways to achieve this. First, we worked hard to strengthen existing alliances, especially with South Korea, Japan, and Australia, and to build political and security relationships with India, Indonesia, and Vietnam. Second, the president was determined to see the United States participate actively in the emerging multilateral institutions of the region, in particular the East Asia Summit.

Third, we wanted to strengthen bilateral and multilateral trade ties with the region through understandings such as the U.S.-South Korea Free Trade Agreement and the Trans-Pacific Partnership.[2] The administration knew that its second year would test the foundations of the relationship it had started to build in the first year.

TAIWAN AND TIBET: CHINA'S "CORE ISSUES"

As 2010 dawned, two immediate challenges presented themselves, with several more lurking predictably right behind. One had to do with Taiwan.

In October 2008 President George W. Bush had approved a $6.4 billion sale of arms to Taiwan that had satisfied Taiwan's principal requirements, so there was no immediate need for the new administration to authorize a further sale. Indeed, Taiwan had not moved even to acquire many of the authorized systems. There was no immediate threat to Taiwan's security in 2009. On the contrary, the mainland and Taiwan had dramatically relaxed tensions and built ties in the year since Ma Ying-jeou assumed the presidency of Taiwan. Direct flights between major cities on the two sides were now occurring for the first time. The two were far along in negotiating a free trade framework agreement, and exchanges of visitors, tourists, and officials had mushroomed.

In any case, the growing disparity between the militaries on the two sides meant it was increasingly unrealistic to think the United States could provide Taiwan with weapons sufficient for its defense. Arms sales served three rather different purposes. One was to provide Taiwan with the wherewithal to withstand a Chinese attack long enough for U.S. assistance to turn the tide. Second, such sales would signal that the United States remained committed to Taiwan's security. Third, they would demonstrate U.S. credibility to other friends and allies in the region who would be alarmed at the use of force in the Taiwan Strait.

There was no serious consideration of a large arms sale before President Obama's visit to China. Not only was there no urgent need, but Assistant Secretary of State for East Asian and Pacific Affairs Kurt Campbell, who was to be a leading figure in decisions on arms sales, was not confirmed until June 2009, which was too close to Obama's visit to justify consideration. But our national security team judged in early 2010 that we should not wait longer to face the arms sale issue, since the obligation to supply arms to Taiwan was a commitment that the United States had to honor, and it would not grow easier with time.

The second sensitive issue was when the president should meet with the Dalai Lama. The president had told Hu, to the latter's displeasure, that he would do so, and I strongly believed it was important to follow through quickly on our promise to meet after the trip and to send a message of our commitment to human rights issues.

Shortly after Obama's visit, the Deputies Committee met under the chairmanship of Tom Donilon to consider our China policy for the first half of 2010 and to make decisions on Taiwan and Tibet. The president also planned to host the first-ever Nuclear Security Summit in Washington in April, an event to which forty-seven heads of state including Hu Jintao would be invited (thirty-eight actually attended).

One item on the committee's agenda was a package of arms for Taiwan prepared by the Defense Department. It included about $3 billion for antimissile Patriot batteries and missiles, $3 billion in Blackhawk helicopters, a feasibility study for the sale of diesel submarines, Harpoon training missiles, and mine-hunting ships. Deputy Secretary of State Jim Steinberg and Assistant Secretary Campbell argued in favor of the sale, though without enthusiasm for the submarine feasibility study (the China-watching security community understood that submarines, no longer manufactured in the United States, would never be sold to Taiwan, whether or not there was a feasibility study). I agreed, and said so. No one argued in favor of the sale of new F-16 fighter aircraft, which President Bush had also refused to sell but which Taiwan and its supporters continued to request.

When it came to the question of whether the president should meet with the Dalai Lama, I was left to carry the burden of the argument, while others showed anemic enthusiasm for the idea at best. Some within the State Department and the White House worried that the combination of the Taiwan arms sale plus the meeting with the Dalai Lama would at a minimum persuade Hu not to come to Washington for the Nuclear Security Summit and perhaps cast a long-term chill over the relationship. These were not unreasonable concerns, since the two issues were precisely the ones that Chinese officials had defined as their "core interests."

Convinced that a presidential meeting with the Dalai Lama was a necessity yet uneasy about the silence from others on the subject, I spoke subsequently to Secretary Clinton and to Presidential Senior Adviser

Valerie Jarrett, who had visited the Dalai Lama in Dharamsala in September 2009. Both agreed that the president should meet with the religious leader in order to follow through on the U.S. commitment, and that the administration should accept the consequences for the relationship with China.

In January 2010 Tom Donilon and I met with the president to go over the arguments surrounding the Dalai Lama meeting and told him that the Dalai Lama was prepared to visit the following month if he agreed. The president, uncharacteristically, interrupted, saying, "Let me cut this argument short. I'm going to meet with him." The president believed that meeting the Dalai Lama was the right thing to do for substantive reasons, and this judgment was reinforced by his assessment of the domestic political damage that would result from further delay. I was pleased and said so. I informed the Tibetans the meeting would take place on February 18.

We then proceeded to a Principals Committee meeting in January to decide on Taiwan arms sales. The Principals Committee was chaired by National Security Adviser General Jim Jones and included among others Secretary Clinton, Secretary of Defense Robert Gates, Chairman of the Joint Chiefs of Staff Admiral Michael Mullen, Director of National Intelligence Dennis Blair, Director of Central Intelligence Leon Panetta, U.S. Ambassador to the United Nations Susan Rice, Tom Donilon, and Jim Steinberg. Their consensus was that the Defense Department's proposed package should proceed and be announced in late January. The Principals Committee endorsed the whole package except for the submarine feasibility study, which the Defense Department representatives said was not in the cards in any event and was inconsistent with the defensive character of the rest of the package.

Congressional notification of the sale was announced on January 29. The next day I had a one-on-one breakfast with a somber Ambassador Zhou Wenzhong from the Chinese embassy. I had known Zhou and worked closely with him since 1995, when he was number two at the embassy. I knew him as someone who could be counted on to recite faithfully and with conviction China's views but who could also work hard to narrow differences and argue with his superiors in Beijing when necessary.

Zhou relayed Beijing's anger over the sale. I asked him if he had noticed not only what was authorized for sale to Taiwan but also what was not authorized. He said he had, absolutely, and believed that would mitigate Beijing's reaction.

We discussed the chances of President Hu's attending the Nuclear Security Summit in April, given the possibility of a presidential meeting with the Dalai Lama in February. Chinese officials had been hinting strongly for some time that the Taiwan and Tibet decisions might make it impossible for Hu to come, and many China-watchers, not to mention senior U.S. officials, were convinced he would not. Zhou was reserved.

Zhou then began to lay out a sequence of steps that he thought might soften the impact of these decisions on relations. A visit by Deputy Secretary Steinberg and me to Beijing was an important first step. After that, the new Chinese ambassador would arrive in Washington. It would be good if the president could meet him and provide authoritative assurances about his attitude toward the relationship. Finally, some sort of public statement by the United States on its arms sales policy that lowered the temperature would be important. I came out of the breakfast thinking for the first time that Hu would in fact come to Washington for the Nuclear Security Summit, that that event could restore positive momentum to the relationship, and that the damage would be relatively short-lived.

In the next few weeks, Beijing's rhetoric over the sale sharpened considerably. It invited American experts on Asia for visits and discussions, and some, though far from all, described dire consequences if Americans failed to accommodate. Egged on by an increasingly nationalistic and vocal blogosphere, Beijing began to threaten retaliation against U.S. companies whose technology or parts were in the Taiwan arms sale package.[3] Among those were Boeing, whose components were a trivial part of the package but which was the largest U.S. exporter to China and a long-term pillar of the U.S.-China relationship. I warned Ambassador Zhou that any retaliation against companies like Boeing would certainly trigger a trade war and major retaliatory actions by the United States, including sanctions against Chinese companies. I did not see a serious prospect of the Chinese carrying through on these threats, but I felt it necessary to nip them in the bud.

Consistent with our kabuki-like diplomatic discussions with the Chinese on Tibet, in late January—before the president's planned meeting with the Dalai Lama was announced—the Chinese held their first dialogue with the Dalai Lama's representatives in nearly two years. The meeting produced no breakthroughs, as Beijing continued to see the Dalai Lama's insistence on recognition of a "greater Tibet" going beyond the borders of the Tibetan Autonomous Region as a disguised independence plot. But the fact that the meeting was held at all was in itself a modest positive sign, one that would not have occurred had the president met with the Dalai Lama the previous October, and it showed that the Chinese had kept up their part of our non-deal deal.[4]

President Obama met with the Dalai Lama on February 18. It was a cordial meeting in the Map Room, one of the ceremonial rooms in the center of the White House where previous presidents had met with him. It lasted for seventy minutes and was marked by the usual unpredictable twists and turns of a conversation with this distinctly nonlinear thinker. The president gave him a copy of a letter that Franklin Roosevelt wrote to the then eight-year-old Dalai Lama in 1943. He told the Dalai Lama that he supported the hopes for genuine autonomy for Tibet so that it could preserve its distinct religious and cultural heritage, reiterated the administration's view that Tibet was a part of China, and urged the Dalai Lama to persist in dialogue with the Chinese and to consider a visit to China if one was offered. The Dalai Lama was warm and respectful, saying that he saw Obama as a tribute to and tribune of American democratic values. The president genuinely liked the Dalai Lama, commenting to me that three iconic figures immediately came to his mind who face-to-face embodied exactly the virtues he anticipated: Queen Elizabeth, Nelson Mandela, and the Dalai Lama.

Providing evidence of the maxim that no good deed goes unpunished, the Dalai Lama walked out the front door of the White House to speak to cameras in front of the West Wing at a prearranged photo op. Because of yet another record snowstorm a couple of days earlier, the cleaning crew had failed to clear out some trash bags in front of the White House, and cameras perched at the West Wing site captured him walking past them. The likes of Rush Limbaugh quickly offered outraged commentaries at this supposed calculated insult, charging that the Dalai Lama was banished to the back door of the White House to appease the Chinese. In fact, he had gone out the front door.[5]

It was only ten days later that Jim Steinberg and I were invited to Beijing for an early March visit. This was not the first trip Steinberg and I took to China together, nor the last. Steinberg was a friend dating back to the

Clinton administration. I had worked for him both at the National Security Council and subsequently at the Brookings Institution and had enormous respect for his intellect, his ability to frame issues with all their consequences, his operational adroitness, and the seriousness with which he studied his brief. Within the U.S. government, he was probably the most skilled analyst of and interlocutor with China, and the Chinese trusted him as someone committed to a constructive relationship who would speak candidly but not hostilely. I was invariably paired with Steinberg on these trips, which we both welcomed. I provided the imprimatur of the White House to Steinberg's presentations, which added authority to their intellectual heft.

It was a rough trip, as we expected. We knew that in all the meetings we would be subjected to theatrical expressions of outrage over our putative violations of China's sovereignty and core interests. But we also knew that our willingness to be there for this ritual was an important part of moving to the next step in the relationship.

At the same time, we were determined neither to simply play defense nor to apologize for actions that we considered proper. Going on the offensive entailed several moves. I assured the Chinese that the president was deeply committed to the relationship with China and had devoted considerable energy and effort into building a positive relationship in the face of some domestic criticism, exacerbated by the maladroitness in China's reception for him during his November visit to Beijing. I expressed the president's dissatisfaction with Chinese economic policy, particularly with regard to the undervaluation of the yuan. We were running an annual trade deficit of well over $200 billion with a country having an undervalued currency and were paying a political price. We pointed to China's foot-dragging on UN Security Council action to impose sanctions on Iran.

In all our meetings, including those with State Councilor Dai Bingguo and Foreign Minister Yang Jiechi, we were subjected to a verbal assault, especially on the subject of Taiwan. Besides ritualistic demands that we halt sales and abide by the terms of the 1982 U.S.-China Joint Communiqué, other proposals were put forward for consultations with China on future sales and for limitations of various kinds on sales. The rhetoric on Tibet was sharp, but lighter and less time-consuming. And in what seemed to us an unwelcome innovation, the Chinese executive vice foreign minister gave a lengthy presentation on China's rights in the South China

President Obama being briefed by Jeffrey Bader, Carol Browner (director of White House Office of Energy and Climate Change Policy), and National Security Council officer Sue Mi Terry before meeting with Prime Minister Kevin Rudd of Australia. (Official White House Photo)

President Obama and Prime Minister Kevin Rudd of Australia walking along the White House West Wing portico during Rudd's first official visit to the White House in March 2009. (Reuters)

President Obama with President Hu Jintao of China at the Pittsburgh G-20 meeting in September 2009, discussing the language for the group's communiqué. (Official White House Photo)

President Obama with President Susilo Bambang Yudhoyono of Indonesia at the G-20 meeting in Pittsburgh, September 2009. (Official White House Photo)

President Obama and Prime Minister Yukio Hatoyama of Japan at a joint news conference at the prime minister's office in Tokyo, November 2009. (Kyodo)

The first meeting of a U.S. president with the ten leaders of the ASEAN countries, Singapore, November 2009. Left to right: Najib Razak of Malaysia, Thein Sein of Burma, Gloria Macapagal-Arroyo of the Philippines, Lee Hsien-loong of Singapore, President Obama, Abhisit Vejja-jiva of Thailand, Nguyen Minh Triet of Vietnam, Sultan Haji Hassan al-Bolkiah of Brunei, Hun Sen of Cambodia, Susilo Bambang Yudhoyono of Indonesia, and Bouasone Bouphavanh of Laos. (Official White House Photo)

President Obama and President Hu Jintao of China at a state dinner during Obama's November 2009 visit to Beijing (Chinese interpreter in middle). (Xinhua)

President Obama addressing a town hall meeting in Shanghai at Fudan University in November 2009. (Xinhua)

President Obama mingling with students at Shanghai town hall meeting, November 2009. (Xinhua)

President Lee Myung-bak of South Korea and President Obama talk to each other, walking toward the venue for luncheon at Cheong Wa Dae (the presidential office) in November 2009. (Yonhap)

President Lee Myung-bak of South Korea and President Obama greet children at a welcoming ceremony held at Cheong Wa Dae in November 2009. (Yonhap)

Last-minute negotiations over the climate change agreement with Premier Wen Jiabao of China (sitting opposite Obama), Prime Minister Manmohan Singh of India (next to Wen Jiabao), President Luiz Inácio Lula da Silva of Brazil (to Obama's right), and President Zuma of South Africa (second to Lula's right), Copenhagen, December 2009. (Official White House Photo)

President Obama at dinner with Prime Minister Yukio Hatoyama of Japan at the Nuclear Security Summit in Washington, April 2010. Prime Minister Hatoyama asked for more time to work out Okinawa basing agreements. (Official White House Photo)

Annual meeting in November 2010 in Yokohama of Asia-Pacific Economic Cooperation Forum. Left to right: President Obama, Prime Minister Naoto Kan of Japan, Prime Minister Lee Hsien-loong of Singapore, Prime Minister Julia Gillard of Australia, Prime Minister Stephen Harper of Canada, and President Hu Jintao of China. (Kyodo)

President Obama in the Oval Office with President Hu Jintao of China during the latter's state visit in January 2011. The visit occurred at the end of a year marked by Chinese international assertiveness and reactions by the United States and countries of East Asia. (Official White House Photo)

President Obama and the author, Jeffrey Bader, with Bader's wife, Rohini Talalla, in the Oval Office, April 2011. (Official White House Photo)

Sea, highlighting this as a national priority (though not, as was publicly reported in the U.S. media, calling it a "core interest" like Taiwan or Tibet).[6]

Steinberg pushed for China to accept an initiative that he had personally conceived and that Secretary Clinton had begun pressing on the Chinese during the Strategic and Economic Dialogue the previous year, namely, a dialogue on sensitive security issues. Participants would be senior civilians and military officials, and their mission would be to deal with subjects most susceptible to leading to conflict: nuclear force modernization, outer space, cyberspace, missile defense, and maritime security. The Chinese, we pointed out, could raise subjects of concern to them in a dialogue of this nature, such as security in maritime areas including the Taiwan Strait. Steinberg made it clear, however, that any discussions touching on the Taiwan Strait could not take U.S. arms sales to Taiwan as their focus but could deal with the balance of forces in the region generally and ways to lower tensions through acts by all, not just by the United States.

We were pressed for assurances that the United States would not sell arms to Taiwan or meet with the Dalai Lama for some specified time frame. We refused to give such assurances.

Shortly after returning to Washington, I met again with Ambassador Zhou. We refined the plan that he had sketched out earlier. The president would meet with the incoming ambassador, Zhang Yesui, and the White House would issue a press release stressing the president's commitment to the relationship and to the administration's "one China" policy with regard to Taiwan. Jim Steinberg would hold a press conference in which he would reiterate the fundamental precepts of the "one China" policy and the U.S. attitude toward arms sales. The Chinese tried to persuade us to share what Steinberg might say, presumably with the intent of trying to edit it. We declined, and Steinberg ultimately gave a press conference on the eve of another trip he was taking, during which he answered a question from a Chinese journalist on Taiwan that fulfilled Chinese expectations in a way entirely consistent with past policy but responsive to Chinese concerns.[7]

Also in early April 2010, much to the relief of the Chinese, Treasury Secretary Timothy Geithner announced that Treasury would not name China as a currency manipulator, as Senators Charles Schumer (D-N.Y.), Lindsey Graham (R-S.C.), and others were demanding. Geithner did not do this as a favor to the Chinese. He thoroughly understood that Washington's ability to persuade China to show more flexibility on the value of the yuan would end the day he declared them a manipulator. Instead, he deferred the decision until after the upcoming IMF and G-20 meetings.[8]

But we were insistent as we approached the Nuclear Security Summit that we would not be dealing exclusively with Chinese concerns. In March, after Ambassador Zhang Yesui arrived, Deputy National Security Adviser Donilon met with him several times to get acquainted and lay out the way forward. Donilon told Zhang that if Hu came for the Nuclear Security Summit, world media attention would be focused on the Iran nuclear issue and on China's attitude toward it. To date, our discussions with the Chinese in the UN Security Council had been fruitless. Now was the time for China to step up and agree to begin discussion on a sanctions resolution. Otherwise, the Nuclear Security Summit would be seen as a setback for U.S.-China relations.

On April 1 the Chinese finally announced that Hu would come to Washington for the Nuclear Security Summit. This was a decision that Hu took personally, over the opposition of some of his colleagues and advisers. His decision was made possible by the sequence of diplomatic steps we had taken since early March: the Steinberg-Bader visit to Beijing, the president's meeting with Ambassador Zhang and the positive White House press release characterizing the meeting, and Steinberg's press conference answer on Taiwan policy. It was a welcome decision, one that indicated that the normal setback to relations after a Taiwan arms sale and meeting with the Dalai Lama would be shorter and less intense than usual.

We continued squabbling with the Chinese over what we might say on Iran up to the moment Hu's plane left Beijing, with the Chinese adamantly refusing to state officially what Ambassador Zhang had been instructed to tell us privately—that China would work with us on a resolution. So upon their arrival in Washington, I called the delegation's Foreign Ministry representative and told him I intended to announce on the record that we had agreed with China to work on an Iran sanctions resolution, and I counted on the Chinese not to contradict that statement. The Foreign Ministry representative called me back an hour later to say they agreed. I did so, to good public effect in major media stories.[9]

I read subsequently a number of blog postings slamming me for making an unfounded statement or betraying Chinese confidence. Chris

Nelson, a well-known Washington daily trade journal publisher who was a sort of founder of blogs before there was such a thing, helpfully published a report saying that a statement by me of such a kind was not a casual or unilateral decision, but something that could only be undertaken with authorization. Nelson was right. That helped shape and produce more informed media discussion of the issue.

President Obama met with Hu for two hours. The meeting went well, producing no negative surprises. Hu did not dwell on either Taiwan or Tibet. Clearly he was looking ahead, not back. The meeting was dominated by two issues of large concern to the administration: Iran and America's economic relationship with China. In the main, the meeting succeeded in closing the chapter behind the two decisions Washington had taken on Taiwan and Tibet, warned Hu that continued inflexibility on the value of the yuan would have consequences, and secured an agreement on working together on a resolution that punished Iran but did not aim at punishing Chinese companies engaged in normal commerce there.

The administration had gone through a trying four-month period, marked by a flood of media articles about rising tensions in the relationship.[10] This media theme replaced the previous narrative that the administration was excessively accommodating Beijing. The apparent inconsistency between these two lines of analysis was squared by implications that the administration had learned the lesson that its accommodation in the first year was wrong, and now it was compensating, or overcompensating. The analysis was mistaken, in my view. The administration had put a necessary floor under the relationship in the first year, avoiding the negative experiences in the transitions of past presidents. That floor had helped Washington weather the difficulties surrounding decisions in early 2010 that were problematic to the Chinese and allowed it to move past these decisions in record time. But a few more difficult months lay ahead.

China's Growing Assertiveness

By the middle of 2010 many China-watchers inside and outside the U.S. government were beginning to write about what they saw as a more assertive China. This was not a dramatically new phenomenon, but the emergence of a somewhat different China from the one the United States had been dealing with for several decades.[11]

Many descriptions of this newly assertive China were overdramatized, and some included irrelevancies such as impoliteness by random Chinese during dinner conversations. Those of us who had decades of experience with China could not recall ever seeing it quietly roll over in the face of foreign demands. China had been truculent in the wake of the Tiananmen massacre, resisting steps that might have made its reintegration into the global community more rapid. The China that fired missiles along the edge of Taiwan and triggered tensions across the strait and with the United States in 1996 was certainly assertive. Americans who dealt with Chinese officials after the accidental bombing of the Chinese embassy in Belgrade in 1999, or the collision of a Chinese fighter jet with an American surveillance aircraft in 2001, did not find China accommodating. Chinese threats to Taiwan's security during the unhappy tenure of Taiwan president Chen Shui-bian had American security officials and analysts on edge.

That said, beginning about 2008 and continuing into 2010 one could detect a changed quality in the writing of Chinese security analysts and Chinese official statements, and in some respects in Chinese behavior. Citing the financial meltdown and subsequent deep recession in the United States in September 2008, some Chinese analysts argued that the United States was in decline or distracted, or both.[12] America's economic strength, the central reason for its global prestige and influence, seemed to be dissolving after several years of massive trade deficits and domestic budget deficits. To finance its debt, the United States was relying more and more on other countries, notably China. Moreover, it appeared bogged down in two wars, in Iraq and Afghanistan, and attitudes toward it throughout the world were the most negative in modern history.

Whereas the United States appeared to be in decline, China appeared to be on the march. It had grown at a rate of more than 10 percent a year for a decade and a half, had sailed through the global recession with minimal impact, and had become the top trading partner of Japan, South Korea, Taiwan, Australia, and India, in some cases supplanting the United States. Its presence was increasingly felt not only in Southeast Asia but also in the Middle East, Africa, and Latin America, where it was no longer a supplicant for investment but an investor in its own right.

The impression that China was rapidly overtaking the United States was rampant not only in Chinese literature but also in American media. Although their analyses properly noted the spectacular changes occurring in China, many lacked depth, seeing in short-term trends developments that would take decades, if ever, to decisively affect, no less overturn, the global balance of power. Many Americans took these comments seriously: according to some polls, a plurality of Americans had come to believe China was richer than the United States (in fact, China's per capita GDP is about 10–15 percent of America's). The perception grew in China as well.

Scholarly articles, media pieces in new nationalist journals like the *Global Times*, and blog postings argued that China's time had come. China should abandon the foreign policy of prudence, caution, and modesty that Deng Xiaoping had championed since 1978, encapsulated in a saying attributed to him: *Tao guang yang hui, you suo zuo wei*, which translates roughly as, "Keep a low profile and take selective actions." Deng had argued that China's overwhelming national priority was internal economic development, and that to achieve this objective it had to enjoy a peaceful international environment. This meant establishing full diplomatic relations with the United States, terminating support for Communist Party insurrections throughout Southeast Asia, deepening relations with Japan, opening up to foreign trade and investment, joining the major international organizations, and adopting the vast array of other policy changes that made possible the Chinese success story that began in the 1970s.

Now, some argued, the world had changed. The correlation of forces in Asia and the world had altered. China did not need to suppress its ambitions. It should assume a leadership role. It should use the leverage provided by its wealth, not least in relation to the United States, which owed it over a trillion dollars. It should utilize the military assets it had begun to develop in the past two decades to project Chinese strength abroad and to undercut American influence.[13]

Chinese scholars who still believed in Deng's precepts were cowed by this rising tide of nationalism. They refrained from challenging what was emerging as the new orthodoxy for fear of both popular onslaughts and official coolness. The public discourse on foreign policy grew increasingly nationalist and one-sided.

This was the context for a number of incidents in the maritime areas surrounding China that created a notably different and tenser diplomatic environment in 2010. These incidents revolved around the Korean peninsula and the Yellow Sea, the South China Sea, and the Senkaku (Diaoyu) Islands claimed by Japan and China, all discussed in the coming chapters.

Some of the incidents in 2009 involved Chinese fishing vessels, which under the guidance of China's navy had confronted U.S. military surveillance ships in international waters within China's 200-mile exclusive economic zone (EEZ). These incidents threatened to escalate, as the Chinese seemed prepared to tolerate risky and unprofessional conduct by their fishing vessels operating under military control or guidance.[14] Beijing contended that foreign military vessels could not operate inside the country's EEZ without its permission. Although a few other littoral states place a similar interpretation on the UN Law of the Sea Convention, the U.S. and overwhelmingly dominant international view is that the treaty imposes no such requirement. Our people spoke to senior Chinese civilian and military officials about the risks a number of times, declined to alter our existing practices, and urged the Chinese to discuss the issue within the U.S.-China Military Maritime Cooperation Agreement forum. By mid-2010 the number of such episodes had fallen off substantially.

EIGHT

Tensions in Korea

THE MOST DANGEROUS challenge the Obama administration faced in Asia in 2010 was not provoked by China, though China certainly played an important role. Rather, North Korea was to blame, with its escalating nuclear and military activities.

When North Korea began its cycle of provocations in 2009 with missile and nuclear tests, Chinese leaders initially stood with the United States in sanctioning the North for these activities. As the year progressed, however, they demonstrated greater solidarity with North Korea, welcoming Kim Jong-il to China on three visits between May 2010 and May 2011. This was probably occasioned by Chinese anxiety over stability in North Korea and fear of its collapse. Kim Jong-il's health and survivability were in question in the wake of his slow recovery from a stroke in August 2008. Economic mismanagement, by no means new, seemed to be threatening stability with a catastrophic currency revaluation in late 2009 that destroyed much of what passed for North Korea's middle class. China seemed nervous about the prospect of a failed state on its border, or perhaps the possibility of its falling into the hands of a South Korea allied with the United States.

In March 2010 a South Korean military corvette-class naval vessel, the *Cheonan*, was sunk in waters near the maritime demarcation line between North and South Korea, killing forty-six sailors. An investigation by six countries, including South Korea and the United States, concluded in

May that the *Cheonan* was sunk by a torpedo fired by a North Korean sub-marine, as clearly indicated by the character of the explosion, the traces of explosive left on the vessel's wreckage, the torpedo shell found near the site of the sinking, and sensitive intelligence.[1] It was not a conclusion the administration assumed from the beginning, nor one that we hoped to reach. The Chinese, on the other hand, questioned the results of the inves-tigation and refused to accept its conclusion that the North Koreans had sunk the ship.

Around the time of the sinking of the *Cheonan*, the U.S. special repre-sentative for North Korea policy, Ambassador Stephen Bosworth, was preparing to meet with one of his North Korean counterparts, Vice For-eign Minister Kim Gye-gwan, in New York. It would have been the sec-ond bilateral meeting between Bosworth and the North Koreans. He had led a delegation to Pyongyang in December 2009 with a view to laying out the circumstances under which the United States could resume negotia-tion to achieve the objectives of the Six-Party joint statement of 2005: denuclearization of North Korea and normalization of the situation on the Korean Peninsula. The 2009 meeting produced no breakthroughs, but it did serve to remind the North Koreans that the U.S. door was open should they decide to take serious steps to denuclearize. The forthcoming meeting, expected in April, would have been a follow-up to the Pyongyang visit.

I was extremely uneasy about the prospect of a Bosworth-Kim meeting at that time. We did not yet have conclusive evidence about North Korean involvement in the sinking of the *Cheonan*. However, in a phone call shortly after the sinking, South Korea's president, Lee Myung-bak, had told President Obama that the cause of the sinking was an externally induced explosion. The evidence seemed to be building that the North was responsible. I felt that a meeting between the lead U.S. negotiator and the North Koreans in the immediate wake of such a provocation by Pyongyang would send a message of indulgence of the North's bad behav-ior and would be badly received in the South.

I asked Bosworth's capable deputy, Ambassador Sung Kim, to check with his South Korean colleagues about their attitude toward a meeting between Bosworth and Kim Gye-gwan. Sung Kim reported back that the South Korean Ministry of Foreign Affairs expressed no reservations. I asked him to double-check. He got the same results.

I then called Jim Steinberg to explain my misgivings. Steinberg agreed wholeheartedly. Since Assistant Secretary Kurt Campbell was to be in Seoul the next day, he suggested I call Campbell to have him take the pulse of the South Koreans. I did so. Campbell called me back the next day to say that he had spoken to senior Blue House (the South Korean equivalent of our White House) officials, who had told him that they would not welcome a Bosworth-Kim meeting. Campbell and I agreed to call it off.

The administration's national security team decided on a series of steps to increase solidarity with the South Koreans in response to the sinking of the *Cheonan*. President Obama spoke to President Lee several times to express U.S. support, to offer assistance in the investigation, and to coordinate further actions toward the North. The two presidents agreed to meet in Toronto at the forthcoming June G-20 meeting and to agree on a number of initiatives to send a strong message to the North. The administration decided to impose new sanctions on Pyongyang and to issue the first executive order specifically targeting the North Korean leadership and entities involved in illicit activities.[2] Previous sanctions had been imposed pursuant to executive orders aimed at nonproliferation activities, but this was a blunter instrument that could be used to target luxury goods and leadership acquisitions more effectively. The Principals Committee decided to pursue action at the United Nations, though our national security team well understood the unlikelihood of obtaining a strong statement. President Obama also decided to inform President Lee in Toronto, and to announce, that the administration was aiming to announce agreement on a revised U.S.-South Korea Free Trade Agreement by the time of the G-20 meeting in Seoul in November.

One other step was particularly important to President Lee, which was to postpone transferring wartime operational control (OpCon) of South Korean forces from South Korean to U.S. command until 2015. In peacetime, South Korean forces had been under the South's command since 1994, but in wartime would still be under the direction of the U.S.–South Korean Combined Forces Command, headed by an American general. Under an agreement negotiated at the behest of former South Korean president Roh Moo-hyun and announced in 2006, wartime command was to be transferred to the South Koreans in 2012. President Lee, supported by many senior retired South Korean generals, felt the transfer had been driven by political considerations and was premature, given the level of

South Korean capabilities. He pledged in his campaign for the presidency to overturn it. President Obama was sympathetic to Lee's concerns. Because of the tensions in the peninsula stoked by North Korea, he also felt that proceeding on the accelerated timetable could be a destabilizing signal. Lee's request for a delay also made an impression on Obama. At a moment when it was imperative to demonstrate the strength of the alliance, it made little sense to have a high-profile disagreement with America's ally over something Lee felt strongly about and on which the administration understood his reasoning.

U.S. Forces Korea, supported by Defense Secretary Robert Gates, were somewhat reluctant to alter the timetable. They had invested four years of planning in the 2012 transfer and did not want to imperil the improvements in South Korean command and control, military acquisitions, and training that were being accelerated by the timetable. The Principals Committee, led on this issue by Secretary Gates, asked Deputy Assistant Secretary of Defense Michael Schiffer and me to work out an announcement of a delay on the basis of South Korea agreeing to acquire the necessary bridging capabilities that would allow the transfer to proceed in 2015 without additional postponement. After working closely with the commander of the combined forces, General Walter Sharp, and with the deputy national security adviser of South Korea, Kim Tae-hyo, we presented Secretary Gates and the South Korean defense minister with a plan for the two presidents to announce agreement on delay of OpCon transfer at their June 26 Toronto meeting, the details to be worked out later.

The United States offered to send its top experts to brief Beijing on the results of the investigation into the sinking of the *Cheonan*. The Chinese refused. They insisted on remaining noncommittal about the cause of the sinking and blocked U.S. and South Korean attempts in the United Nations to unambiguously identify North Korea as the responsible party.

When President Obama met with Hu Jintao on June 24 at the G-20 meeting in Toronto, they had a sharp exchange on North Korea. President Obama told Hu that failing to acknowledge North Korean aggression would enable the North to do more of the same. Hu gave a bland response stressing China's evenhandedness in dealing with North and South Korea. The response clearly irritated Obama, who went back at the subject, warning of the potential consequences to regional peace if China tolerated North Korea's aggression. In a press conference later that day, while expressing understanding of China's restraint in approaching the North given its position on China's border, Obama took the unusual step for him of complaining about what he described as China's "willful blindness" and misguided evenhandedness.[3]

After the Obama-Hu meeting in Toronto, Washington persuaded the Chinese and the Russians to agree to a presidential statement by the UN Security Council that deplored the attack, noted the investigators' conclusion that North Korea was responsible (though including reference to the North Korean denial), condemned the attack, highlighted the importance of preventing future attacks on the South, and called for honoring the armistice. In "UN-speak," the short shrift given to the North's denial alongside detailed reference to the investigation's conclusion of North Korean responsibility, and the Security Council's condemnation of the "attack," signified the council's acceptance of Pyongyang's responsibility. But the American and South Korean media treated the statement's failure to unequivocally censure North Korea as a defeat.[4]

In response to the sinking of the *Cheonan*, the United States and South Korea also decided on a series of joint military exercises to demonstrate our deterrent power against North Korea. One exercise was to be a U.S. aircraft carrier deployment off South Korea's coast. In July the South Korean press reported that the United States intended to deploy the carrier U.S.S. *George Washington* to the Yellow Sea, between Korea and China. The report was based on a leak of contingency planning within the U.S. Pacific Command, not on any decision to deploy forces there, for in fact no such decision had been made.

The report infuriated the Chinese press and blogosphere. Retired admirals and generals wrote that such an exercise along this "historical invasion route" to Beijing constituted a direct challenge to China that needed to be confronted. More troubling, China's Foreign Ministry representative warned that such a deployment in sensitive waters near China could threaten Chinese national security.[5]

At a subsequent Deputies Committee meeting in late July, members decided that the carrier group should be deployed to South Korea's east coast, not the Yellow Sea. The principal reason was that the United States wanted to send an unambiguous message of deterrence against North Korea, without confusing the message with different signals. I strongly concurred with this decision. In my view, a further North Korean provocation was likely before long and would amply justify a subsequent deploy-ment to the Yellow Sea in order to send the right message not only to the North Koreans but to the Chinese. North Korea's earlier provocations had begun in April 2009 with its ballistic missile test and continued through the nuclear test and the sinking of the *Cheonan*. This pattern of behavior was consistent with the North's past conduct. Whenever it has sought attention and rewards from the United States and South Korea, it has resorted to incitements of this nature. Still in its early fragile stages, the leadership transition from Kim Jong-il to his son Kim Jong-un reinforced this pattern. During this transition, the elder and younger Kim were likely to continue to seek opportunities to visibly demonstrate their toughness.

On November 12 the North Koreans showed what they described as a uranium enrichment facility to visiting U.S. nuclear scientist Siegfried Hecker, former head of Lawrence Livermore National Laboratory. Hecker could not determine whether the facility was operational, but he was impressed by its sophistication. This confirmed long-standing U.S. suspicions that North Korea had successfully developed another method for producing nuclear weapons besides its plutonium production facility, validating the intelligence that led to the breakdown of the Agreed Framework in 2002.[6]

President Obama met with Hu Jintao at the G-20 meeting in Seoul in November, shortly after the administration heard about Hecker's findings in North Korea. Obama warned Hu that the situation in Korea was mov-ing in a dangerous direction. He pointed out that the combination of North Korea's ballistic missile program, its development and testing of nuclear weapons, its newly announced uranium enrichment facility, and the leadership's belligerence in the midst of an uncertain transition posed a threat not only to peace, but also to American national security. Obama said America's strong preference was to work with China to defuse the North Korean threat. But if cooperation could not succeed, the president said he would not hesitate to do what was necessary to protect U.S. national security. Hu seemed taken aback by the substance and sharp tone of the presentation, moving off script to ask for details of what Obama was describing.[7]

On the same trip, Obama met with South Korea's president Lee Myung-bak in Seoul. The meeting dealt in large part with the status of the U.S.–South Korea Free Trade Agreement, on which the two sides had failed to come to terms. That failure dominated media coverage of the trip, which roundly criticized President Obama for it. (Characteristically, the U.S.–South Korea agreement three weeks later on terms more favorable for the U.S. automobile industry than would have been obtained in Seoul triggered considerably less media interest.) But the two presidents also talked about the North Korean threat at some length and in complete alignment, with Obama privately telling a pleased Lee that the United States intended to send the carrier U.S.S. *George Washington* into the Yellow Sea within the next ten days.[8]

On November 23, in response to a South Korean live-fire exercise, the North shelled the South-administered island of Yeonpyeong, near the maritime demarcation line and not far from the site of the sinking of the *Cheonan*. Four South Koreans were killed, including the first civilians killed by the North in a military attack on Korean soil since the Korean War.

In the immediate aftermath of the Yeonpyeong shelling, the U.S.S. *George Washington* was deployed to the Yellow Sea. The administration had long ago decided that such a deployment was necessary, on a date to be determined, in order to signal that we would not be intimidated by Chinese Foreign Ministry warnings contrary to the Law of the Sea Convention. The brazenness of the shelling muted even official Chinese reactions to the deployment.

The deployments culminating in the Yellow Sea exercise sent an important message to Beijing: North Korean provocations would induce U.S. and South Korean responses not at all to their liking. Washington hoped this would encourage China to restrain North Korea in the future.

In late November, Jim Steinberg and I were once again dispatched to Beijing to make sure the message was fully understood. We reiterated that the president wanted to work with China to denuclearize North Korea, but that U.S. national security interest was affected and the president would act to protect it. We added that the Yeonpyeong attack and the South's weak response had had political repercussions as President Lee had fired his defense minister and made clear that China could expect a South Korean military response to future provocations by the North. That meant it was critical for China to do all within its power to restrain North Korea.

We rejected China's proposal for an emergency meeting of the Six Parties, whose proper goal was to deal with the North Korean nuclear issue, not North-South tensions. The urgent priority at the moment, we pointed out, was for the North to make amends for its multiple provocations through direct talks with the South. We also rejected the idea that North Korea should be allowed to trigger a meeting of the Six Parties, whose goal was to deal with denuclearization, by undertaking an act of aggression while flaunting new nuclear weapons production capabilities.

The Chinese continued to urge patience with the North and restraint on all sides, but they now understood that the time for indulgence of the North had passed. Within days, China's foreign minister issued a statement calling for North-South talks. State Councilor Dai Bingguo made it clear that he took the new situation very seriously and traveled to North Korea to warn Pyongyang not to react to ongoing South Korean exercises.[9]

Dai's trip was especially important in light of the fact that while Steinberg and I were in Beijing urging China to restrain North Korea, the South Koreans announced that they would conduct another live-fire exercise on Yeonpyeong Island, the same kind of exercise to which the North had reacted by shelling Yeonpyeong. This was a regular exercise during which forces would fire in a direction arguably less problematic than in October but would show by proceeding that the South would not be intimidated. With tensions running high, however, the U.S. side was concerned the situation could escalate uncontrollably unless it made clear to the South Koreans what kind of action the United States could support and what kind it could not.

In a heated discussion in mid-December, the Deputies Committee debated whether to try to persuade South Korea to abort the exercise, and how far to go in that endeavor. The South Koreans were considering retaliation well beyond a local response. They also seemed prepared to delegate authority to local commanders to undertake a disproportionate response that might have triggered a North Korean artillery barrage in populated areas. Some in the Deputies Committee argued that a live-fire exercise at that moment, when the U.S.S. *George Washington* was steaming into the Yellow Sea, was unacceptable and should not receive U.S. support of any kind. Others, while skeptical of the exercise's value, felt everything possible should be done to ensure that the risk of escalation was limited, but that the United States could not fail to provide support for it. The latter view, which I favored, prevailed.

In order to limit the risks, we decided to convey several key points to the South Koreans. We would make clear that U.S. forces were providing logistical and intelligence support. We would also ensure that our public messaging was fully supportive. Chairman of the Joint Chiefs of Staff Michael Mullen was sent to South Korea to deliver a message of strong U.S. support, while seeking to ensure the South Korean operation did not lead to escalation.

Tensions were still high as the exercise unfolded. On the night of December 19, Denis McDonough gathered Danny Russel, members of the National Security Council's Defense Directorate, and me in the Situation Room, with a direct link to the Pentagon's National Military Command Center to monitor the exercise and the North Korean response. As the exercise unfolded, it appeared that at least one artillery shell had landed in waters claimed by North Korea. We began wondering whether we would see a repeat of the November 23 shelling or worse. At 2 a.m., a couple of hours after the exercise was completed, we knew we could go home, comfortable that there would be no escalation.

The North Korean provocations of October and November tested the Obama national security team's revised approach, with competing objectives that needed to be pursued simultaneously. We wanted to demonstrate to the North Koreans that provocations could no longer trigger the old cycle of extortion followed by reward. We wanted to demonstrate support for the South, which meant not only enhanced sanctions against the North but also working with the South to send a message through military exercises, deployments, and preparations. We also wanted to work with the Chinese to restrain North Korea, but we would first have to persuade Beijing that Pyongyang's behavior constituted a threat to Chinese interests. We would also have to ensure that the package of new sanctions, exercises, threats, and a tougher South Korean military posture did not cause Pyongyang to overreact and incite uncontrolled escalation.

The results of the October-November actions reflected, and generally vindicated, this approach. The administration refused to go back to Six-Party Talks or put forward a new package of incentives for North Korea. The administration made clear that Six-Party Talks would resume only when North Korea took the necessary steps to provide confidence of its seriousness about denuclearization, notably a freeze on nuclear tests, a freeze on ballistic missile tests, a verifiable freeze on its claimed uranium enrichment program as monitored by International Atomic Energy Agency (IAEA) inspectors, a commitment to the 2005 joint statement, and a pledge to honor the Korean War Armistice. Heartened by U.S. support, the South agreed to scale back its more aggressive plans for retaliation in November and to begin contemplating talks with the North that could ease tensions. The Chinese weighed in heavily with the North to counsel restraint during the second round of South Korean live-fire exercises and shifted their own position away from immediate Six-Party Talks and toward the North-South talks that the United States favored. The North in turn began moving toward a resumption of talks with the South. Then it shifted 180 degrees away from its earlier assertion that the Six-Party Talks were dead and buried forever.[10]

By the end of 2010 we felt we had sent the strongest possible message that we would not resume the old cycle, and that North Korea needed to adjust. It was not clear, however, that the North would comply. For decades, its leaders have single-mindedly pursued a nuclear weapons program. Their tactics have shifted, but their goal has not.

We understood that simply breaking the cycle would not achieve the administration's objectives. Many of us believed that the most likely long-term solution to the North's nuclear pursuits lay in the North's collapse and absorption into a South-led reunified Korea. But that belief is not a sufficient basis for dealing with a short- and medium-term threat. A strategy was still needed to slow down, freeze, and degrade the North Korean program until history could take its course.

By the end of 2010 the stage seemed reasonably set for the next steps in pursuing an effective "freeze and degrade" strategy, but the drama was still to play out. The South and the North had begun secret contacts aimed at a plan for reducing tensions. The North hoped to parley the talks into monetary, food, and energy assistance from the South and to weaken their archrival, Lee Myung-bak, in the process. For its part, the South sought to end North Korea's belligerence, to persuade the North to take steps to denuclearize before any assistance could be provided, and to find ways to encourage it to move toward democratic reunification through penetration of its closed society. This promised to be a long, drawn-out process.

Meanwhile, the Obama administration was prepared to contemplate a resumption of bilateral talks with North Korea once South Korea indicated it was satisfied the North had provided adequate assurance that there would be no further military provocations. Bilateral talks between the United States and the North would be aimed at laying out the conditions under which Six-Party Talks could resume and Washington could implement the 2005 joint statement goals of denuclearization, normalization of relations in the Korean Peninsula, and assistance to the North.

In early 2011 our team held a series of quiet consultations with the key South Korean officials involved in North-South talks. The South's internal politics on North-South issues are historically secretive and byzantine. President Lee holds all the strings, while different actors in the Blue House, the National Intelligence Service, and the Foreign Ministry are allowed to play out their roles in compartmentalized fashion. We wanted to make sure we knew who was doing what, so that our own policy would be coordinated with what Lee was doing. To that end, Denis McDonough and CIA director Leon Panetta hosted the director of the National Intelligence Service, Won Sei-hoon, on a visit in February 2011, and key Blue House adviser Kim Tae-hyo visited soon thereafter for talks with McDonough and me. The South's chief negotiator, Vice Foreign Minister Wi Sung-lac, also arrived for talks with State Department and White House counterparts.[11] McDonough made clear the Obama administration's unflinching support for President Lee and South Korea, as well as the expectation that their approaches on both North-South and on nuclear issues would be closely coordinated. We came out of this series of talks with agreed-upon objectives and rough timelines, but no certainty that North Korea would be willing to accept a constructive process.

NINE

BUILDING STRONGER TIES
WITH SOUTHEAST ASIA

FROM THE TIME of Secretary of State Clinton's first trip abroad, which included Indonesia, the Obama administration had wanted to signal that our interests in Asia went beyond the traditional American focus on Northeast Asia. Attention would also be given to the countries of the Association of Southeast Asian Nations (ASEAN), Australia, and New Zealand. With a population of 600 million, an increasingly integrated market, and some of the world's most dynamic economies, Southeast Asia plays a huge role in the global economy. Furthermore, it lies at a strategic crossroads between two large rising powers, China and India, and astride the waters plied by many of the world's petroleum shipments. Much of the region felt neglected by the Bush administration. Secretary Clinton's trip to Indonesia, her visit to ASEAN headquarters, the decision to accede to the ASEAN Treaty of Amity and Cooperation, and the appointment of the first-ever Jakarta-based U.S. ambassador to ASEAN, all mentioned earlier, were the administration's first steps toward closer ties with ASEAN.

For the better part of a decade, the relationship with ASEAN had been held hostage to Washington's Burma policy. Ruled by a brutal military dictatorship, Burma, now called Myanmar, is a xenophobic, closed country that has stood out as a failure amid a group of regional success stories. From the time that Burma joined ASEAN in 1997, U.S. administrations had leaned on the association to press Burma to reform lest ASEAN be tainted by its failings. This policy produced meager results. ASEAN tried to encourage engagement with Burma and urged patience, but Burma's ruling junta refused reform. At the same time, China, and to a lesser extent India, were making inroads in Burma, which all the while was developing a military relationship with North Korea. Judging that Burma was of minimal strategic importance, a succession of U.S. administrations essentially gave stewardship over Burma policy to the human rights community, which prescribed its traditional medicine of name and shame, sanctions, isolation, and threats to invoke the International Criminal Court. There was no indication that such a policy was any more effective in bringing about reform than Washington's six-decade embargo against Cuba had been, but a succession of American administrations showed no political will to alter the policy, and frankly no alternatives were likely to have a short-term positive impact.

Over the course of the next two years, the Obama administration endeavored to elevate Washington's relationship with Southeast Asia to a higher level. It introduced six initiatives to this end.

First, U.S. policy toward ASEAN would no longer be held hostage to Burma. Washington would continue to urge reform in Burma, arguably more effectively, by developing a relationship with ASEAN at senior levels without putting the organization in an impossible position of having to choose between the United States and one of its members. In a significant break from policy during the Bush administration, President Obama authorized opening a diplomatic dialogue with Burma to see if the United States could affect its behavior at home and abroad. Assistant Secretary of State Kurt Campbell was put in charge of the dialogue. Although progress at the outset was slow, as expected, Burma's junta did agree to free opposition leader and democratic icon Aung San Suu Kyi from house arrest in November 2010, opening up possibilities for opposition activity that were previously unavailable.[1] Campbell consulted closely with Aung San Suu Kyi at each step of our dialogue with the junta to ensure her support.

Second, President Obama decided to hold regular annual meetings with the heads of the ten ASEAN countries. President George W. Bush had considered such a meeting toward the end of his administration but ultimately dropped the idea owing to unease about meeting with the ASEAN ten with Burma in attendance. Under Obama, the National Security Council staff and the State Department were assured by the

ASEAN countries that Burma's dictator Than Shwe would not be present, but that its prime minister would attend in his place. We decided not to hold ASEAN responsible for its most objectionable member, and to meet with the ten ASEAN leaders with a lower-ranking Burmese participant. Obama held his first meeting with the group in Singapore on the margins of the Asia-Pacific Economic Cooperation (APEC) meeting in November 2009. He held a follow-up meeting with it at the UN General Assembly in September 2010 and intends to continue the practice.[2]

Third, the administration had an intensive internal debate over whether the president should join the East Asia Summit (EAS). The State Department strongly favored joining, whereas economic agencies felt it would undercut APEC and be redundant. Many in the White House also opposed EAS membership for straightforward scheduling reasons, out of concern about committing the president to two Asia visits each year. When this objection was raised at one interagency meeting, I suggested that in 2010 Secretary Clinton attend in the president's place as an observer, paving the way for his attendance the following year. I chaired a succession of interagency meetings in which we thrashed through the issues, ultimately producing a memorandum laying out the options for the president to decide.

Tom Donilon, who saw a stronger U.S. presence in Asia as a central feature of Obama's foreign policy, favored joining the EAS. Given the degree of confidence the president had in Donilon's judgment, his position on the matter carried considerable weight.

I spoke to President Obama about the EAS at the G-20 meeting in Toronto on June 27, 2010, after his breakfast with Indonesian president Susilo Bambang Yudhoyono. He had urged President Obama to join the EAS, echoing the strong pitch that Australia's prime minister Kevin Rudd had made during his meeting with the president in January 2010. If the United States joined, reasoned the president, it could affect the evolution of the EAS. He felt the organization could not develop into a serious and constructive player on political and security issues if the United States stayed outside. I was of the same opinion and mentioned the option of Clinton attending that year. Several days later, Donilon told me that the president had decided to join. Secretary Clinton rearranged her schedule with some difficulty to permit her to attend in 2010, her second visit to Hanoi in just over two months.

Fourth, the administration had to articulate a serious policy to expand trade, both with Southeast Asia and more broadly throughout the world. Because of strong reservations in the Democratic congressional caucus, the administration had been slow to move forward on finalizing and ratifying free trade agreements, particularly the one with South Korea negotiated by the Bush administration. But by 2010 the Obama administration had begun to move away from a purely rhetorical commitment to trade toward a more activist policy. In their June 2010 meeting in Toronto, Obama told South Korea's president Lee Myung-bak that he wanted to complete the agreement by the time of his November visit to Seoul. That target was missed, however, primarily because of continuing disputes over the pace of further opening of the U.S. market to Korean automobiles, but the problem was overcome and agreement reached three weeks later, paving the way for ratification in 2011.

In conjunction with that decision, Obama announced his commitment to negotiate a model free trade agreement with the other members of the Trans-Pacific Partnership (TPP): Australia, New Zealand, Singapore, Chile, Brunei, Vietnam, Malaysia, and Peru. The United States convened a meeting of the heads of state of the TPP countries at the APEC gathering in Yokohama in November 2010 to highlight the negotiation and its goals. Intriguingly, though not yet part of the TPP, Japan, APEC's host, asked to join the meeting, while Prime Minister Naoto Kan spoke publicly of his country's desire to become a member of the partnership. Many remain skeptical about whether Japan will be able to make the market-opening commitments required by the TPP, but the goal of membership may spur it finally to make the hard decisions to open its agricultural market, which it has resisted for a generation.[3]

Fifth, the United States sought to build a deeper relationship with ASEAN's leader, Indonesia. The most populous and powerful country in ASEAN, Indonesia was a charter member of the newly created G-20, slated to replace the G-8 as the most important multilateral grouping of the world's major economies. Indonesia had surprised virtually everyone by building a stable functioning democracy in the decade since President Soeharto was ousted in 1998. The world's largest Muslim-majority democracy, Indonesia had fought aggressively and effectively against al Qaeda affiliates in its midst after the Bali bombing in 2002, to the point where Indonesia was widely cited as a possible model for Middle East Arab countries later undergoing revolution and reform in 2011.

On an institutional level, Washington established a so-called comprehensive partnership with Indonesia involving linkages between multiple agencies on both sides that increased assistance for education, health, clean energy, and climate change mitigation in Indonesia. In a politically difficult decision that pitted the administration against elements in the human rights community and Congress, the administration also sought modest cooperation with Kopassus, the Indonesian army's principal counterterrorist arm.[4] Kopassus had been guilty of massive human rights violations under Soeharto in putting down unrest in East Timor in the late 1990s. Since then, it had been rebuilt almost from scratch with an entirely new officer corps as well as a reconstituted rank and file trained by Australian and European forces to respect human rights and humanitarian law. The president of Timor-Leste, Nobel Peace Prize–winning Jose Ramos-Horta, who had greater moral credibility concerning Indonesian abuses in East Timor than anyone in the West, urged Washington to lift all sanctions against Kopassus, arguing that the new, reformed, democratic Indonesia and its army did not need to be burdened by ghosts from the past. I chaired several contentious interagency meetings, which led us to conclude that a relationship with Kopassus was permissible under U.S. law if the Indonesians agreed to certain commitments. Defense Secretary Robert Gates and Joint Chiefs of Staff Chairman Michael Mullen pushed hard to open the door to cooperation with Kopassus, with the support of Secretary Clinton (though not all in her chain of command). With considerable help from the government's leading officials for human rights, Assistant Secretary of State for Democracy, Human Rights, and Labor Mike Posner and Senior Director for Democracy Samantha Power of the NSC, commitments were secured from the Indonesian leadership that made it possible to move past this outdated restriction and begin building ties with the military's chief counterterrorism instrument. Though a small step, this was a very important signal to President Yudhoyono and his government that Obama was prepared to take on politically difficult issues for the sake of the relationship.

To signal the new relationship, the president decided early on to visit Indonesia, where he had lived as a child. Unfortunately, the trip seemed to be snake-bit. It was originally planned for March 2010, but the key vote in the House on the Obama administration's health care plan was due precisely when the president planned to travel. With his signature domestic proposal at stake, Obama judged he had to postpone the trip (and along with it a planned trip to Australia). It was rescheduled for June 2010, but that date turned out to be equally problematic. BP's damaged Deepwater Horizon well was gushing oil into the Gulf of Mexico, and the president could not be seen as traveling abroad at a moment of domestic crisis.

Obama had breakfast with President Yudhoyono in June 2010 in Toronto to explain the delay in his travel and to commit to the relationship. The meeting demonstrated in a modest way the special quality of what Obama brought to the Indonesia relationship. When the Indonesian press came in for a photo session as breakfast was beginning, Obama greeted them with several sentences in Bahasa, Indonesia's language. The press responded enthusiastically in unison. Obama leaned over to Yudhoyono and said, "I speak Bahasa with a perfect accent," which struck me as uncharacteristic boastfulness until he immediately added, "But I have the vocabulary of a six-year-old," which was his age when he had lived in Indonesia. Obama told Yudhoyono that he intended to visit Indonesia at the first opportunity but could not yet commit to a date.

In November the president planned a trip to India, South Korea (for the G-20 meeting), and Japan (for the APEC meeting). There seemed little time for an additional stop, and little enthusiasm in the West Wing for one in the wake of what the president described as a "shellacking" in the November congressional elections. But he was determined to visit Indonesia and managed to find time between the India and South Korea stops. The streets en route from the airport to the palace in Jakarta were lined with people several rows deep waiting in a driving rainstorm to greet the president. When he spoke at the University of Indonesia, an enthusiastic crowd welcomed him as if it was a homecoming. He was presented with a special medal by Yudhoyono honoring the work of his mother in creating microcredit institutions in Indonesia. With expected presidential visits in 2011 (for the EAS) and 2013 (for APEC), the U.S.-Indonesia relationship was well on its way to the higher level Obama sought.

In addition, the administration confronted some challenges in the nation's relationships with its other three Asia-Pacific allies—Australia,

Thailand, and the Philippines—and with Malaysia, Singapore, and Vietnam. In the case of Australia, these consisted of opportunities rather than problems. Prime Minister Kevin Rudd and President Obama had developed a close relationship in the course of several face-to-face meetings that revealed their shared cerebral approach to policy, wonkish fondness for complicated issues, and calm demeanor. Rudd played an important role as a "thought partner" for Obama on issues such as the East Asia Summit, the G-20, and climate change. He also committed to increasing the Australian contingent in Afghanistan by 40 percent shortly after Obama took office, making Australia the largest contributor to the military effort there outside of NATO. After Rudd was ousted in an internal coup in the Australian Labor Party in June 2010, Obama quickly developed a warm relationship with his successor, Julia Gillard, who was invited to Washington for an Oval Office meeting in March 2011. In addition to the foregoing benefits, the relationship produced conversations about how to increase U.S. military deployments and exercises in Australia that culminated in an announcement in November 2011 of U.S. plans to deploy Marines on a rotational basis to northern Australia for joint training exercises.

By contrast, Thailand presented more problems than opportunities. In 2006 former prime minister Thaksin Shinawatra had been ousted in a military coup quietly supported by the royal family. The Thaksin administration had been thoroughly corrupt, and he was loathed by Thailand's Bangkok-based elite and middle class, but his populist policies had strong support in Thailand's poor rural areas. Since his ouster, no Thai government had been able to acquire legitimacy derived from democratic elections, and in 2010 Thailand ground virtually to a halt for months because of mass demonstrations by so-called Red Shirts funded by and supportive of Thaksin. During the demonstrations, some within the State Department wanted to open contacts directly with Thaksin, then living in Dubai. I opposed such contacts, saying we should reach out to Red Shirt leaders but not to him personally. At the time, he was a fugitive wanted by the Thai Ministry of Justice for corruption and was fomenting violence designed to overthrow the Thai government. Any contact with him would inevitably become known to the Thai government and would be seen as an unfriendly act. I thought that if and when the opposition returned to power, U.S. evenhandedness and respect for Thai law would prevent damage to our relationship.

In fact, Thaksin's party won a decisive electoral victory in July 2011, after I left office, elevating his sister to the position of prime minister.

I also resisted well-intentioned proposals by our ambassador to Thailand and midlevel State Department officials to become involved in some form of mediation, judging that we had no significant leverage and would only discredit ourselves by participating in a process without results. Whatever the deficiencies of the Thai regime, it still had the support of the parliament, the royal family, and the military, and it worked well with Washington on a number of important nonproliferation actions, including the seizure of an aircraft trying to carry North Korean weapons to the Middle East and extradition of one of the world's leading arms smugglers. At the same time, the Obama administration did not want to embrace a government lacking in popular support and electoral legitimacy, so it never held a presidential one-on-one meeting with Thailand's prime minister. Instead, it took clear public positions condemning violence by either side, unconstitutional actions or threats to law and order, and violations of human rights. But Washington worked closely with the Thai government at lower levels, waiting for elections expected in 2011 to produce what it hoped would be a government supported by a national consensus.

The administration had no urgent matters to attend to in the Philippines. President Obama met with President Gloria Arroyo in the Oval Office in 2009, and then with her successor, Benigno Aquino, in New York in 2010. One issue that came to interagency attention during my tenure was a contingency plan within U.S. Pacific Command (PACOM) to draw down its special forces operating against the Abu Sayyaf group and other terrorists in Mindanao in 2009. We decided to delay any drawdown, both as a demonstration of our continued forward deployment in the Western Pacific and our resolve to eliminate the terrorist threat emanating from southern Mindanao. Considerable progress against Abu Sayyaf had all but eliminated it, reducing it to a group of armed robbers and extortionists without international reach.

Malaysia was a signal success story for the Obama administration. Then deputy prime minister Najib reached out to the campaign in 2008, asking to meet with me during a visit to the United States. We had a warm conversation that convinced me his orientation toward the United States would be entirely different from that of his predecessors if he became prime minister. When he did succeed in reaching that position, early on Najib signaled significant changes in Malaysia's domestic and foreign policy. He began reforms to open up Malaysia to foreign investment and trade, asking to join the Trans-Pacific Partnership trade negotiations. Working with U.S. experts, he pushed through an export control law designed to end Malaysia's reputation as a sieve for sensitive technologies destined for countries like Iran. He courageously decided to send a battalion of Malaysian military doctors to Afghanistan, making Malaysia the third Muslim-majority country to deploy forces there. President Obama recognized this was an opportunity for a different kind of relationship with Malaysia. He called Najib in 2009, and Najib was one of very few heads of government that Obama met with at the Nuclear Security Summit in April 2010. More recently, Najib has become an important voice against extremism in the Muslim world.

As for the U.S.-Singapore relationship, it did not need to be reinvented, only nurtured. Singapore was a long-standing friend that for decades had provided crucial diplomatic and military support, particularly for the U.S. Navy and its visiting ships. In October 2009, as a sign of respect for Singapore, Obama met with its founder, Lee Kuan Yew, in the Oval Office. Obama recalled that in his youth Lee was held in great esteem, bordering on awe, in Southeast Asia. In November 2009 Obama visited Singapore for an APEC meeting and met with Prime Minister Lee Hsien Loong, for whom Obama also had high regard. Washington relied heavily on Singapore for advice on issues like the East Asia Summit, trade, the South China Sea, and a host of other regional security and economic issues.

Of all the countries in the region, Vietnam was arguably the most determined to see the United States play a greater role there because of its anxiety over China. While not wishing to be drawn into Vietnam-China arguments or to take a position on their respective claims in the South China Sea, the administration welcomed an enhanced relationship with Vietnam and its support for the U.S. presence. The administration sent Secretary Clinton to Vietnam twice in 2010, welcomed it into the TPP trade negotiations, and collaborated with Vietnam to advance the international community's interest in the South China Sea (see chapter 10 for further discussion of this subject).

All in all, the Obama administration sought a greater presence in Southeast Asia at a time when the region was finding its place in an emerging world order between a rising China and a rising India. The purpose was not to pursue zero-sum rivalry with China but to be an active player in the region, lest the United States be seen as an increasingly irrelevant power. The ties that the Obama administration built up with the countries of the region were important to anchor U.S. presence and interests more firmly. This became apparent in July 2010 at the ASEAN Regional Forum meeting where the South China Sea was a featured subject. No one in the region, with the possible exception of Vietnam, wished to see the United States embroiled in a confrontation with China. But all of the countries wanted it to be significantly present as China rose. Improved relations presented important bilateral opportunities, but also served a strategic purpose.

TEN

CHINA'S PUSH INTO
OTHER MARITIME AREAS

As THE OBAMA administration was moving ahead with a new policy in Southeast Asia, its relations with China encountered some unexpected turbulence. In early 2010, I read a State Department press guidance issued following an incident between Chinese and Southeast Asian fishing vessels in the South China Sea. The gist of the guidance was that the United States took no position on territorial claims to islands in the South China Sea asserted by China, Vietnam, Philippines, Malaysia, Taiwan, and Brunei. While that statement was true, it seemed to me to leave out a host of other considerations important to U.S. interests in the region and to send a message of passivity about U.S. rights. After discussing the matter, Assistant Secretary of State Kurt Campbell and I decided to convene an interagency group meeting on the South China Sea, which I chaired.

RHETORICAL SQUARE-OFF ON THE SOUTH CHINA SEA

Evidence laid out at the meeting demonstrated that Chinese naval deployments in the South China Sea had increased markedly since 2000. Incidents between Chinese and other claimant states also were on the rise. China already had a history of pressuring and intimidating energy companies seeking contracts with Vietnam to explore for oil and gas in the South China Sea. I recalled the increasingly strong articulation of China's "indisputable claims" in the area that I had heard during my visit to Beijing with Steinberg in February 2010, as well as occasional assertions by military and midranking civilian officials to the effect that these waters were of "core interest" to China. Campbell and I decided that a new, more comprehensive articulation of U.S. policy was called for.

Campbell and his staff drafted a statement for Secretary Clinton to deliver at the annual meeting of the ASEAN Regional Forum (ARF) in Hanoi in July 2010. He and I contacted other delegations in the twenty-seven-member forum to urge them to speak about international rights in the South China Sea. Secretary Clinton's draft statement reiterated the long-standing U.S. position of not taking sides on territorial claims. At the same time, it asserted vital American interests such as freedom of navigation, the expectation that all claims to rights in waters in the South China Sea would need to be grounded in land-based claims valid under the Law of the Sea Convention, free commerce in the region without intimidation, support for a collaborative process to resolve competing territorial claims, and U.S. willingness to facilitate negotiation of a binding code of conduct for the area. The statement never mentioned China, restricting itself to principles.[1]

Secretary Clinton delivered her formal statement containing these principles in Hanoi at a closed-door session of the ARF, and she outlined its key points in a subsequent press conference. A dozen other countries spoke at the meeting on the issue, some forcefully, especially in the case of Vietnam. China's foreign minister, Yang Jiechi, waited till the end and then delivered a twenty-five-minute stem-winder that shook the meeting from its usual torpor. Staring directly at Secretary Clinton for much of the time, he denied that there were any problems in the South China Sea and warned ASEAN countries not to become involved in a cabal organized by an outside power. He told the Vietnamese representative that as a fellow socialist country, Vietnam should not side with a country that considers *socialism* an epithet. At one point, he exclaimed, "China is a big country. Bigger than any other countries here." From its intimidating tone, the address was clearly meant to deter the ASEAN states from seeking outside or multilateral support.[2]

Yang's speech marked a high point in China's year of assertiveness that left many outsiders wondering if his remarks signaled a turn toward greater muscularity in Beijing or instead would lead to a sober reflection on whether public belligerence really served China's interests. Within weeks, Chinese officials and scholars confirmed the latter was a more likely outcome, putting out word that China had not authoritatively called the South China Sea a "core interest," as asserted in the U.S. media.[3] By September, as President Obama was preparing to meet with the ten leaders of the ASEAN countries, China indicated that it was willing to begin expert talks on a code of conduct in the South China Sea. While meetings so far have proceeded slowly, with agreement on such a code still some distance off and incidents in the South China Sea continuing, the resumption of quiet diplomacy signaled Beijing's awareness that assertiveness in the area had its costs.

CHINA-JAPAN SHOWDOWN OVER UNINHABITED ROCKS

To add to the tensions surrounding the South China Sea spat and China's alignment with North Korea, a new maritime incident in September 2010 sparked further friction in the region. It had to do with what Japan calls the Senkaku Islands and China calls the Diaoyu Islands, a group of uninhabited rocky islets in the seas west of Okinawa. Both Japan and China had long laid claim to the islands, although Japan had effectively controlled and administered them since Okinawa had reverted to Japan in 1971.

On September 7, 2010, the Japanese Coast Guard chased off a score of Chinese fishing vessels operating close to one of the Senkakus—not a particularly unusual event, except that one of the Chinese fishing vessels disregarded the warnings. Piloted by a captain the Japanese later found to be drunk, the boat struck two Japanese Coast Guard vessels. Instead of following their usual practice of simply throwing the captured ship's fish back into the sea and sending the boat and its crew on their way, the Japanese treated the incident as a dangerous provocation and hauled both the boat and its crew into custody in Japan.

Owing to their history of hostility over much of the twentieth century, China and Japan easily succumb to nationalist passions whenever a bilateral incident takes place, especially one that entails territorial disputes and arrests.[4] After holding the crew for a few days, the Japanese released them all except for the captain, announcing he would be subject to a judicial proceeding. That decision suggested Japan was treating this as a law enforcement issue within its jurisdiction, not a diplomatic incident. The

Chinese reacted sharply. Senior officials condemned Japan's action and warned of grave consequences. Their reaction went beyond statements: four Japanese businessmen in western China were arrested, and leaked reports indicated that so-called rare earth minerals, vital for Japan's electronics and digital product assembly, were no longer being shipped from China to Japan. Since China has been the source of over 90 percent of the world's rare earth production, this was a serious problem.[5]

On September 23 President Obama and Secretary Clinton were in New York for meetings on the margins of the UN General Assembly, which for the first time included talks with Prime Minister Naoto Kan and Foreign Minister Seiji Maehara. The Senkakus incident had created a complex dilemma for the administration. Under the U.S.-Japan Treaty of Mutual Security and Cooperation of 1960, the United States was obligated to defend all territories administered by Japan, which clearly included the Senkakus. On the other hand, the United States did not take a position on the respective territorial claims of Japan and China over the Senkakus. Although Washington wanted to show solidarity with its ally Japan in the face of bullying, Japan's handling of the incident seemed maladroit. Above all, it was absurd to think that China and Japan could have an armed conflict over these rocky islets or that the United States would be drawn in. As a result, the administration hoped for a rapid de-escalation before both sides were drawn into further provocations by angry publics.

Kurt Campbell and I met with senior Chinese and Japanese officials in advance of Clinton's and Obama's meetings to explore modalities to resolve the situation. When Secretary Clinton met with Foreign Minister Maehara and asked about the case, he told her the captain's release was imminent and Prime Minister Kan would deliver the news to Obama. Kan in fact did so, and Obama expressed satisfaction with the plan.

Before the release, Chairman of the Joint Chiefs of Staff Mullen, Secretary Clinton, and I spoke publicly, reaffirming the U.S. obligation to defend all areas administered by Japan, including the Senkakus. Mullen said, "Obviously we very, very strongly support our ally [Japan]." In my press briefing after the president's meeting, in response to a question about possible war, I described our obligations under the treaty, our silence on the territorial dispute, and the absurdity of any suggestion that a military conflict between China and Japan over the Senkakus was on the horizon and that the United States would be drawn in.[6]

Although there was enough blame to go around, this was yet another incident that ended up harming China's image more than anyone else's. In the eyes of the world, China seemed prepared to upend global trading arrangements and practices (regarding rare earths) in retaliation for what looked like a bilateral dispute and to give it international consequences. Foreign analysts wondered openly how the Chinese would react if other countries cut off resource exports to them. For its part, Japan began approaching numerous countries about the prospects for new sources of rare earth minerals.

ELEVEN

THE ROAD TO HU JINTAO'S VISIT TO THE UNITED STATES

OVER THE COURSE of 2010, China's incautious and gratuitously assertive diplomacy and actions had alienated most of its neighbors, notably Japan, South Korea, Vietnam, Indonesia, and India. Relations with the United States had also become more complicated. Instead of building a peaceful environment in its neighborhood, China seemed to be encouraging creation of a belt of hostile states on its periphery, all seeking—and in fact developing—closer relations with the United States.

The third pillar of the Obama administration's Asia strategy had been to ensure that China's rise contributed to, rather than detracted from, regional stability. A principal means to this end was to strengthen U.S. alliances and partnerships in the region to assure countries there that China's rise would not come at their expense. The assumption of our national security team was that they would naturally feel a certain degree of anxiety about China's growing power and thus would welcome a U.S. presence and forward deployment.

But for much of the previous decade, China had played its cards well, expanding trade and investment links with others in the region and generally enhancing its soft power. Indeed, a rich literature had emerged about countries like South Korea and others in Southeast Asia being inevitably drawn into China's sphere of influence. What happened instead was that China began to clumsily alienate its key neighbors. Yet its foreign policy analysts confused cause and effect and blamed the United

States for the deterioration in China's relations with its neighbors. China's policies had actually made the United States more welcome in the region and tilted relationships there away from China, as reflected in the strengthened U.S. relations with Japan, South Korea, India, Indonesia, and Vietnam.

Although misguided, China's leaders were fully capable of correcting their mistakes. Behind the scenes, there was intensive introspection about the shortcomings of their policy.

In their meeting in June 2010 at the G-20 in Toronto, President Obama had invited Hu Jintao to the United States for a state visit, reciprocating Obama's visit to China the previous November. High-level visits with Chinese leaders are seldom politically popular at home, and it was not a universally welcome decision in the West Wing to invite Hu for a state visit no less. But the president continued to believe that the U.S.-China relationship was key to achieving his principal foreign policy goals, and he was prepared to take risks to his popularity at home in order to build it.

Since the Chinese attach considerable importance to protocol, ceremony, form, and appearances, they invariably expect all such visits to be designated as state visits. When Washington attempted to arrange a working visit by then president Jiang Zemin in 1995, for example, the plans were aborted because China insisted it should be a state visit despite the U.S. judgment that the fragile relationship at that time did not warrant such status. (He eventually made a state visit in the fall of 1997.) In 2006 President George W. Bush invited Hu for a visit, but in deference to China-skeptics within his administration, he declined to call it a state visit and withheld the normal honor of a state dinner. The Chinese nevertheless described it as a state visit, but snafus and disruptions during the welcoming ceremony left the delegation, especially President Hu, angry and dissatisfied.

Although President Obama recognized that a state visit would attract greater scrutiny, and criticism, than a lower-profile visit, he decided this was necessary to advance the relationship. We wanted to give Hu a better reception than he had received in 2006, but also wanted to ensure that public messaging about the visit avoided the misperceptions surrounding Obama's November 2009 trip. But that required dealing not only with the security issues that had dominated the work of my office, but also with the problems in U.S.-China economic relations that were an even bigger political headache.[1]

ECONOMIC IMBALANCES

When President Obama came into office in 2009, China was running close to a $200 billion annual trade surplus with the United States. Over the previous decade China had become the fastest-growing large market for U.S. exports, while the United States had become a kind of vacuum cleaner for low-cost Chinese products. On a purely bilateral basis, the Chinese surplus threatened to stretch out for years to come. In order to reduce inflation at home, China took the dollars garnered from sales to the United States out of circulation, reinvesting those export earnings massively in U.S. Treasury instruments, so that by 2009 its U.S. Treasury holdings topped $1 trillion. China's willingness to buy U.S. debt was welcomed by the Treasury, but according to many economists it had an overall negative effect since it helped hold down interest rates artificially and thus facilitated the amassing of excessive debt and issuance of bad loans, which contributed to the meltdown of the U.S. financial system in 2008. To add to these concerns, many Americans, particularly in the Midwest and in the trade union sector, believed that U.S. companies were closing down and moving to China to take advantage of cheap labor to manufacture products sold back into the U.S. market. With unemployment moving past 10 percent within months after Obama took office, the widespread belief that American jobs were being lost to China was a potentially explosive factor in U.S. politics and in the U.S.-China relationship.

According to many American politicians and respected economists, Chinese exports had gained a competitive advantage in U.S. and other overseas markets largely because Beijing had not allowed the yuan to trade at market levels (though the disparity between the U.S. and Chinese savings rates was actually more important). Early in the second Bush administration, Congress was already considering proposals to retaliate, either by imposing a straight 27.5 percent tariff on all Chinese imports (as suggested by Senators Charles Schumer and Lindsey Graham) or by building into the computation of duties in trade remedy cases under U.S. law a supplement for the amount of the yuan's undervaluation. There also was a steady cry each April, before the annual U.S. Treasury report was issued, to designate China a currency manipulator. Such a move would not have had much practical effect, since it simply would have compelled the United States to begin consultations with China to resolve the issue. But as a practical matter and without visible dissent in the administration, Treasury Secretary Timothy Geithner argued that China would not only refuse to negotiate under such circumstances but also would probably slow or halt the appreciation of its currency.

Between 2005 and 2008 China had allowed its currency to rise in value by about 20 percent, which relieved some of the pressure at that time for U.S. retaliation. But with the financial meltdown and uncertainty over the state of the global economy, China halted upward revaluation in 2008. So U.S. pressure for retaliation resumed.

Currency undervaluation was but one factor that tilted the playing field in favor of Chinese companies over foreign competitors. China also provided a range of subsidies to domestic companies in order to build them into national champions. At the same time, it forced foreign investors to transfer technology, thereby reducing or eliminating their competitive advantage. The U.S. business community was particularly alarmed by China's "indigenous innovation" policies, under which government procurement plans gave preference to innovative products of domestic companies. Violations and piracy of intellectual property rights by Chinese companies and citizens also were rampant, to the detriment of foreign patent and copyright holders in information technology, pharmaceuticals, publishing, chemicals, automobiles, and many other sectors.

Since economic recovery was President Obama's highest priority upon taking office, a principal question he asked his advisers was how U.S. China policy could contribute to the recovery of some of the 8 million jobs that had been shed in late 2008 and early 2009. He was not satisfied that the invisible hand of international economic theory would achieve this goal, and he pressed his team for different approaches.

I became acutely aware of the president's concerns in this regard one day in late 2009 when I came in to brief him on what was billed as an overall China policy session. Invariably, the president allowed his briefers to begin by laying down their analysis. This session was different. Before I could begin, President Obama said he wanted to describe his perspective. He had recently had lunch with four chief executive officers who had spent most of the time complaining about Chinese practices: violations of intellectual property rights, discriminatory actions by regulators, and favoritism for domestic companies. The economic relationship with China was somewhat like a basketball game, he said. For years, we used to trounce them, so if they threw a few elbows around in the lane it didn't matter, we could ignore it. Now the game was much closer, and they were continuing to throw elbows around, but the referee wasn't calling any fouls. So he wondered if we didn't need to find a way to push back, to start throwing around a few elbows ourselves.

I replied that I was entirely comfortable with pursuing a tougher trade policy on China. We needed, however, to be sure that the steps we took did not hurt us substantially if and when China retaliated. I suggested that we could be more aggressive in initiating actions against China under World Trade Organization (WTO) rules, and in utilizing other instruments available under U.S. law consistent with the WTO to bring cases against Chinese companies. The cases that industry leaders had brought to his attention were real and disturbing but had been around for many years, over a decade in some cases, I said, and in some instances had much more to do with the interests of U.S. investors in China than export opportunities. I also suggested that if the president decided to launch a tougher trade policy, the business executives who were urging him on today would vanish tomorrow. As usual, the president listened respectfully, and he laughed at my comment about the business executives, but he was obviously unconvinced.

Over the course of 2010, the president and his top economic advisers had frequent intensive discussions about China economic policy. The meetings were generally moderated by National Economic Council Director Larry Summers and included Larry's deputy Mike Froman, Treasury Secretary Geithner, Tom Donilon, Treasury Under Secretary Lael Brainard, National Economic Council Senior Director David Lipton, and me.

Summers and Geithner were critical of the direction the Chinese economy had taken in recent years and were disturbed by the impact of its discriminatory practices on U.S. competitiveness. In a series of meetings and memos to the president, they laid out the scope of the harmful practices China was engaged in, and the consequences of each. They proposed a

mild

variety of options to consider, from relatively anodyne to draconian ones. These included increased bilateral and multilateral pressure on China to appreciate its currency, aggressive use of China-specific Section 421 of the Trade Act of 1974 to prevent surges of imports, sanctions against companies that had engaged in intellectual property rights violations to prevent them from investing in the United States, WTO cases against a variety of offending practices, designation of China as a currency manipulator, pursuit of a WTO case alleging China's currency was undervalued (with or without a Treasury designation), and either support or passivity (rather than opposition) in the face of various congressional bills that would retaliate against China.

Summers and Geithner were in no way apologetic for Chinese practices. Indeed, they both wrestled with proposals to satisfy the president's evident interest in a tougher trade policy. But at the end of each discussion or memorandum, they consistently concluded that the impact of China's practices on the U.S. economy was in fact quite small, and that even positive corrections would have considerably less impact in the United States than most people imagined. They also foresaw considerable risk of Chinese retaliation, mobilized by a state less bound by international rules and practices than the U.S. government was, that would cost us more than it would cost China. And they pointed out the potential reactions of markets to the appearance of protectionism by the administration.

As a result, their recommendations tended to focus on ways to persuade China to increase the value of its currency, which they thought had the greatest potential to contribute to U.S. economic health, although more aggressive use of Section 421 might also be considered. It had been utilized in 2009 against surges in imports of Chinese tires but was not used more frequently because only a few U.S. companies had sought to petition under this provision. Finally, the president's team decided to keep an open mind on various pieces of proposed legislation regarding currency, depending on whether the Chinese were taking steps to address the problems.

As the administration headed into the second half of 2010, with the prospect of a Hu Jintao visit, the president and his key advisers were increasingly convinced that the visit and our China policy would be judged substantially by the degree to which we were able to aggressively defend American economic interests. We also foresaw a substantial risk that legislation aimed at China, perhaps destructive legislation, might pass and the president not be in a position to veto or shape it.

DONILON AND SUMMERS VISIT BEIJING

In July 2010 Tom Donilon spoke to me about the possibility of his going to Beijing, primarily to prepare for Hu Jintao's visit. At the time, Donilon was deputy national security adviser. It was an open secret that he was likely to become national security adviser by the end of the year. In many ways, particularly in briefing the president daily and in chairing the interagency deputies process, Donilon was already acting as a kind of shadow national security adviser. Given the deep involvement of national security advisers in relations with China—Henry Kissinger, Zbigniew Brzezinski, Frank Carlucci, Brent Scowcroft, Tony Lake, and Sandy Berger, all of whom had visited China—I thought it was a good idea. Donilon had a keen interest in China and wanted to play a central role in developing relations with it. I had met Donilon in 1995, when, as chief of staff to Secretary of State Warren Christopher, he had been key in shifting the Clinton administration's China policy away from its hitherto unsteady course. So I encouraged him.

Later in the month, Donilon told me that he was thinking of taking the trip along with Larry Summers as a way to emphasize the two dominant elements in the relationship, the security and the economic, in the same meetings. He thought that having the president's key White House advisers on these sets of issues visit China would communicate a level of presidential concern and interest in the relationship as it sailed through some rough waters. It was a unique pairing for such a trip, but it made sense.

The Chinese knew of Donilon's likely elevation. He had played a central role in laying out to the Chinese the circumstances under which Hu Jintao was able to visit Washington for the Nuclear Security Summit in April. They also knew of Summers's leading role in the White House on economic policy. So they agreed to the visit without hesitation. A schedule was worked out for the first week of September, ruining Labor Day weekend for the traveling team—Donilon, Summers, Kurt Campbell, National Security Council China director Evan Medeiros, aides to Donilon and Summers, and me.

Our goal was to begin laying out substantively what was needed to make the Hu state visit a success from our perspective. We knew that it would be a lightning rod for critics of China and of U.S. policy. During Obama's trip to China the previous November, official discussions had gone well, but we received a public thrashing because of unrealistic expectations, incorrect or distorted characterizations of what happened, preordained media narratives and myths, and some sloppy messaging on our part.

The Donilon-Summers trip was also to convey authoritatively to the Chinese leadership a sense of the kind of relationship Obama sought. He wanted them to understand that he did not see the relationship in zero-sum terms, and that he was interested in building its cooperative elements. These intentions had been drowned out on both the Chinese and American sides in media pronouncements about tensions at high levels and disputes over Korea, Iran, Taiwan, Tibet, climate change, maritime issues, the yuan's value, access to China's market, Chinese Internet repression, the hacking of U.S. corporate intellectual property, and human rights. The Obama administration wanted to make clear to the Chinese that it cared about these issues and had expectations about how to address and manage them, but it did not want problems to pass a tipping point and feed hostilities on both sides.

The Chinese saw the Donilon-Summers visit as an opportunity to right the somewhat unsteady ship on their side. They arranged a very impressive schedule of meetings with China's top leaders: President Hu Jintao, Premier Wen Jiabao, Vice Premier Wang Qishan (who oversees the economy and finance), Politburo member and Organization Department head Li Yuanchao, State Councilor Dai Bingguo, Foreign Minister Yang Jiechi, People's Bank of China governor Zhou Xiaochuan, and Central Military Commission vice chairman General Xu Caihou. I had asked Ambassador Zhang Yesui to give us a schedule that included a senior leader, a future leader, a senior military officer, top foreign policy officials, and top economic policy officials. He gave us all of them, and then some. It was apparent the Chinese placed great stock in the visit.

Donilon began each meeting with a description of Obama's global foreign policy goals, the higher priority the administration placed on Asia, and the place of China policy in his overall strategy. Repeating what Obama had said to Hu, he declared China's support was critical for achieving their shared goals in combating the proliferation of weapons of mass destruction in Iran and Korea, preventing war on the Korean Peninsula, combating terrorism and stabilizing Pakistan, creating global stability, and turning back climate change. He pointed out the risks and impact on each side's national objectives if their relationship became defined by distrust. President Hu's trip presented an opportunity to put the relationship on a solid track for the remainder of the Obama presidency, Donilon said, noting the alternative would be to dig a hole that would be a struggle to get out of. On specific issues, Donilon spelled out what was needed for Hu's trip to be seen as a success from the U.S. perspective:

—The administration was pleased with China's support for the recently passed UN Security Council Resolution 1929 imposing new sanctions on Iran. To keep the pressure alive, it was important that China not make new energy investments in Iran. Since China was Iran's largest investor in the energy sector, that would send a powerful message, especially now that European, Japanese, and others had withdrawn from Iran's energy sector.

—Further pressure needed to be exerted on North Korea to avoid future provocations such as the sinking of the *Cheonan* and to persuade North Korea to commit to serious progress on denuclearization.

—It was essential for China to unequivocally endorse the referendum on southern Sudan's independence, to honor the outcome, and to use its influence in Khartoum to prevent subversion of the referendum process.

—High-level military-to-military exchanges should be resumed by China agreeing to a visit by Defense Secretary Robert Gates to Beijing. Military-to-military relations had been suspended in the wake of the administration's January 2010 announcement of an arms sale package for Taiwan. If the militaries of these two great powers were isolated from each other, Donilon warned, it could only lead to tension and ultimately confrontation. In the Obama administration's view, military-to-military relations were not a favor to one side or the other, but their joint responsibility as major powers.

In Larry Summers's presentations, the Chinese heard a display of brilliance, history lessons, economic theory, and trains of logic and quasi-geometric proofs that tested the limits of the interpreters' skills. The essence of his message was that China and the United States were faced with mirror-image problems. China was a society that saved too much, spent too little, provided little in the way of a safety net for its citizens, and compounded the problem by unwise currency policies. If China failed to allow its currency to appreciate, he said, it was inviting inflation, which would affect its competitiveness as much as the foregone revaluation and bring other social ills along with it. The United States, on the other hand, saved too little, spent too much, and faced both fiscal and economic recovery problems. China and the United States would be doing themselves, but also each other, a favor by adopting sound policies that addressed these problems. If they failed to do so, there would be heightened pressure in the United States for policies of retribution against China.

The Chinese reaction in all the meetings was a steady drumbeat of references to their desire for cooperation with the United States. By the time we left, even Donilon knew the Chinese word for cooperation, *hezuo*, having heard it many times. Little was said about Taiwan and even less about Tibet. The meeting with Li Yuanchao featured a lengthy personal presentation explaining in detail why China would not challenge the United States for global leadership and why there was no inevitable conflict in their interests. On the last night of the visit, Donilon and Dai had a lengthy exchange about North Korea in a teahouse adjoining Tiananmen Square, with Dai insisting on China's unyielding opposition to North Korea's nuclear weapons program. The meeting with Wen Jiabao featured the sharpest presentation on Taiwan arms sales (presumably his assignment) and pushback on the yuan revaluation argument, prompting a spirited rejoinder from Summers. General Xu said China agreed that military-to-military relations should be restored and would arrange for Gates to visit China at an appropriate unspecified time (Xu caught us all off guard by presenting Donilon with a china plate bearing a lifelike portrait of Donilon, causing considerable mirth in the U.S. delegation). Hu Jintao was particularly warm and welcoming, indicating publicly in front of the cameras (for the first time) that he looked forward to accepting Obama's invitation to visit the United States.

At the end of the meetings, I met privately with a Chinese vice foreign minister and told him we were inviting Hu to visit the United States on January 18–20. He said his office would get back to me soon with a response.

REFINING THE MESSAGE, AND THE MESSAGING

Shortly after the Donilon-Summers trip, the administration began holding interagency meetings to determine what could be accomplished during Hu's visit, and how to frame the public messaging around it. The meetings were chaired by Tom Donilon, Deputy National Security Adviser for Strategic Communications (and speechwriter par excellence) Ben Rhodes, and me. We concluded that the administration was achieving varying degrees of success on three baskets of issues, and we needed to figure out where we could push and how to characterize what we were doing.

First, on political/security issues, we had a good story to tell. The Chinese had done the principal things the administration was looking for on Iran: they had supported a strong UN Security Council resolution on sanctions, had frozen new energy investments, and had participated positively in the negotiations with Iran undertaken by the so-called P5 + 1 nations (the five permanent members of the UN Security Council—the United States, United Kingdom, France, China, and Russia, plus Germany). On Korea, the picture was mixed: China had supported strong action in response to Pyongyang's nuclear and missile tests but more recently had failed to condemn North Korea for its sinking of the *Cheonan*. The administration wanted to improve that record in the time before Hu's arrival. On Sudan, China had endorsed the UN referendum in South Sudan and said it would honor and support the outcome. Military-to-military relations were about to resume, with Secretary Gates due to visit China ten days before Hu's visit. The U.S. pushback on Chinese overreach in the South China Sea and the Yellow Sea, through Secretary Clinton's statement in Hanoi and our military exercises with the South Koreans, seemed to be having some effect on Chinese behavior and rhetoric.

President Obama's decision to join the East Asia Summit signaled an increasing U.S. presence in the region. The marked improvement in relations with post-Hatoyama Japan and agreement on a plan for the Futenma Replacement Facility (despite continuing uncertainty over implementation) shored up Washington's principal alliance in the region. Secretary Clinton was planning a trilateral meeting with the foreign ministers of Japan and South Korea in early January 2011, which would send another strong message of allied solidarity in the face of North Korean provocations. Finally, the president was preparing for a November trip to India, Indonesia, South Korea, and Japan, four of the major countries in Asia troubled by China's assertive policies and all of which were improving relations with the United States The overall picture, then, was one of a strengthened U.S. position in the region, and more constructive Chinese behavior in no small part because of that, as well as a stable U.S.-China political/security relationship featuring close and frequent consultations at the highest levels from the president on down.

As for the second basket, consisting of economic issues, the record was mixed. Since June when the Chinese had announced they would resume "reform of the currency regime," the value of the yuan had crept up 0.5 percent a month, more than before but less than Washington was seeking. The Chinese were also beginning to respond to pressure to revisit their "indigenous innovation" policies, and they agreed in December to treat foreign innovative products the same as domestic ones. In addition, they agreed to require all state and state-owned entities to use only legally produced and acquired software and to provide funding to them to do so. The administration pushed for a number of major commercial deals in the run-up to the visit, and the Chinese agreed to a buying mission that traveled to major U.S. cities and signed contracts immediately before the visit.

In the case of the third basket, human rights, there was no good news. The Chinese leadership had reacted sharply to the Nobel Committee's decision to award its 2010 peace prize to leading dissident Liu Xiaobo, who was serving the first year of a thirteen-year sentence for sedition. They had shown no disposition to release Liu or other high-profile dissidents, including several public interest lawyers, detained in recent years whose cases U.S. officials had highlighted. The last round of Chinese dialogue with the Dalai Lama's representative had occurred in January 2010, and a new round was not in the offing. While people's lives in China were undoubtedly improving and ordinary citizens had more control over their lives as a result of economic advancement, liberalizing systemic reform was not occurring, and the protection of civil liberties was at best frozen.

The overall strategy for Hu's visit, then, was not so much to achieve new "deliverables" but to advance on a few key issues, and to tell the story of what the administration had achieved in the previous two years more effectively. We would describe fairly and without embellishment our assessments of the state of play on the three sets of issues. And we would work overtime to avoid marring the visit with the kind of protocol insults that Hu Jintao had experienced during his 2006 visit, to ensure that the

Chinese leader would go home with a sense of satisfaction that the relationship served his political needs as well.

AFTER HESITATION, HU DECIDES TO VISIT

The first challenge was to secure Chinese agreement on the date we had suggested for the visit. My proposal of January 18–20 was initially greeted with positive signals on the Chinese side. Indeed, the Chinese ambassador informed us in late October that those dates would work, and we began working on a schedule for a visit to Washington and Chicago in that time frame. However, China's chief of protocol visited in late October and informed his counterpart that those dates were not agreed to at senior levels and could not be considered definitive. This news seemed nonsensical, since the Chinese ambassador would not have taken it upon himself to confirm the dates to us. So I pestered the Chinese ambassador every few days for a reconfirmation of the dates, thinking the problem might simply be poor communication on their side.

When they failed to reconfirm in a week, it was apparent that the problem ran deeper. I surmised that it might have something to do with the upcoming Nobel Prize presentation ceremony on December 10, as well as legislation under consideration in Congress that would impose duties on Chinese goods because of the undervalued yuan. In addition, the Korea issue had heated up considerably in October and November, with the North Korean announcement of its uranium enrichment program and the shelling of Yeonpyeong Island. I concluded that the Chinese might be having second thoughts about the visit and were waiting to see how these issues played out before committing themselves. It still seemed manifestly in Hu's interest to proceed with the visit, to demonstrate his sound management of China's most important relationship in his next-to-last year as general secretary, but Chinese leadership politics were too opaque for us to be certain of this.

The ice broke in December. In a fit of self-induced paranoia, some Chinese officials convinced themselves that Secretary Clinton had called the Nobel Committee to direct the awarding of the prize to Liu Xiaobo, and that either President Obama or Secretary Clinton would break all precedent and visit Oslo for the December 10 ceremony. None of this was based in fact. The president issued a warm statement welcoming the award for Liu and included a tribute to the courage of activists for human rights, but neither he nor Secretary Clinton went to Oslo.[2]

With the Republican takeover of the House of Representatives after the November 2010 election, the incoming chairman of the Ways and Means Committee overseeing trade legislation did not consider punitive legislation on the yuan a high priority. At the time, the Chinese were busy in Washington taking the legislative temperature, as well as assessing the administration's attitude, and they concluded, correctly, that the chance of legislation on the yuan before Hu's visit was minimal. Hu certainly did not want to visit on the heels of congressional action, so assurance on this score was essential to his proceeding.

Also worrying were the events in the Korean Peninsula in October and November (described in chapter 8). We told the Chinese, particularly during the visit Steinberg and I made to China in November, that North Korea's uranium enrichment program and its military provocations against the South would be the dominant political issue during Hu's visit and a lightning rod for criticism of China if it continued to remain silent. Tom Donilon reinforced this message in a series of meetings with China's ambassador to the United States.

Although not apparent then, it is evident in retrospect that the Chinese were debating the direction of Chinese foreign policy in the last few months of 2010. For most of the year, the advocates of a more assertive Chinese policy (see chapter 7) had gone unchallenged publicly, while those favoring the more traditional cautious foreign policy had been effectively silenced.[3] However, 2010 did not play out as the advocates of assertiveness had expected. Japan did not continue its 2009 drift toward China but instead moved back to strong and open solidarity with the United States in reaction to North Korean and Chinese actions. Chinese indulgence of North Korea had not weakened the U.S. position on the peninsula—on the contrary, it had strengthened U.S. ties with the South and profoundly damaged China's relations with Seoul. Because of China's aggressiveness in the South China Sea, relations with its Southeast Asian neighbors, principally Vietnam and Indonesia, also suffered. Relations with India were problematic as well. In the wake of Obama's November tour of China's neighbors and his warm reception in each capital, China began reflecting on the unhappy state of its own relations with its key neighbors, except for North Korea and Burma. This record prompted a concerted pushback against the advocates of unnuanced assertiveness.

This change in course became public in early December, when State Councilor Dai Bingguo published a lengthy article on the Foreign Ministry's website (subsequently reprinted in *People's Daily*) offering a resounding defense of Deng Xiaoping's traditional policy of prudence, modesty, and caution (*Tao guang yang hui*) in foreign policy. China's interests had been well served by this policy, said Dai, as it had laid the basis for China's spectacular economic growth and emergence on the international stage. It would be counter to China's interests, he added, to abandon this approach in favor of seeking to become a superpower, a hegemonic power, or a peer competitor of the United States. Dai's article obviously was intended to be an authoritative rebuttal of the public narrative dominated by hard-liners. Dai had the support of Hu Jintao for this strong public position. It amounted to a rebuke of those who had been arguing for a more assertive policy toward the United States, and it emboldened others to call for a more moderate regional diplomacy. It simultaneously provided official justification for a more accommodationist approach toward the United States.[4]

By early December these various points of friction—Korean Peninsula tensions, congressional consideration of China legislation, the Nobel Prize ceremony, and the internal debate over assertiveness—had reached a decisive point, and Dai's article represented the verdict. Hu judged that China needed to demonstrate to the international community not its aggressiveness, but its sense of responsibility. He decided, apparently over some internal opposition, to proceed with his visit to the United States. The Chinese ambassador called me on December 12, two days after the Nobel ceremony, to say he had instructions to confirm that the visit would go ahead on January 18–20.

THE FINAL PLANNING STAGE

With the Chinese having delayed a final decision on dates until December 12, and with decisionmaking in Washington slowed by the pre-Christmas to New Year's vacation period, we had just over two weeks to pull together the most important remaining substantive pieces for the visit. The first concerned economic issues. Secretary Geithner and Tom Donilon concluded by late December that further Chinese movement on the yuan was not imminent, yet the administration did not want the Hu visit to be judged exclusively by the value of the yuan. Although we continued pushing the Chinese on revaluation, we broadened the agenda and worked to shape the public debate on economic issues related to China around a larger set of themes. If one combined the appreciation of the yuan with the difference in inflation rates, Geithner argued, China's inflation rate, exceeding the American rate by about 4 percent, effectively made China about 10 percent less competitive than the United States than it had been in June 2010. He also shifted the U.S. objective more toward market access issues in China, noting in a speech he gave in early January that U.S. exports to China were "growing at twice the rate of our exports to the rest of the world," and that U.S. economic equities in the relationship were bound up in continuing that trend.[5] Finally, the administration pressed the Chinese to agree to sign a number of big-ticket contracts with U.S. companies, foremost among them Boeing, General Electric, and Westinghouse.

Second on the agenda were political/security issues. If Hu were to arrive as an apologist for North Korea just after its uranium enrichment program had been revealed, the visit would be a catastrophe. Kurt Campbell was put in charge of negotiating yet one more joint statement, which was to be issued during Hu's visit. Donilon and I instructed Campbell to make the Chinese understand that the language on North Korea was the make-or-break requirement of the joint statement. Absent satisfactory language on North Korea, the Chinese would be told there would be no statement. Their strong desire for a statement gave the administration useful leverage and made the threat credible. And we fully intended to follow through, although we recognized that the tactic would not escape criticism if it failed to produce a statement.

Finally, there were the countless protocol and logistics arrangements required to ensure a satisfactory visit. These had been the downfall of Hu's 2006 visit and had complicated Obama's trip to China in 2009. We in the White House were determined to avoid those mistakes. When the Chinese asked several times if questions could be avoided at the joint press conference, as in 2009 on their home turf, I told them there would definitely be questions, with two for each president. As for the location of the arrival ceremony, we knew weather in January was a risk and an indoor event would be more modest and less susceptible to disruption, but we decided to go with the outdoor option. We went over the names in the press corps to ensure no fake journalists were present who might disrupt the ceremony, as in 2006. I personally reviewed the cue cards given to the announcer to avoid any repeat of the mistake made by President George W. Bush's announcer, whose cards had been prepared by a White House intern and referred to China as the "Republic of China" (Taiwan's official name). The heads of American and Chinese companies participating in a business roundtable event with the president were also subjected to excruciating due diligence and review by White House staff, as were the dinner guests.

I reached a breaking point with the vetting process when the White House lawyers questioned the suitability of Jackie Chan to attend the dinner. I felt I had a stake in it, having put Chan's name on the list. I had to fight a rear-guard battle when their Google search through 40 million "Jackie Chan" entries turned up reports of Chan fathering a love child with a young Hong Kong actress and making unflattering remarks about the readiness of Chinese citizens for democracy. I pointed out that Jackie Chan was an actor, not a politician, and that no one cared about his political views. As for his liaison with an actress, I said that is what most people expect of actors. Moreover, Chan was the single best-known person of Chinese ethnicity on the planet, and without a doubt the most popular Chinese in both China and the United States. I didn't feel the need to play my trump card, that President Obama was a huge fan of martial arts movies and doubtless would be incredulous if we excluded Chan. Reason prevailed, or at least I did, and Chan attended the state dinner, attracting lavish and positive attention from attendees and the media and no inquiries about his political views.

Ten days before Hu arrived, Secretary Gates finally went on his long-delayed visit to China, marking the full restoration of military-to-military ties. Gates was received at the highest levels and treated well. He was satisfied with his visit, his discussions, the agreements reached, and his reception. The one negative incident was the Chinese test of a J-20 stealth fighter aircraft during his visit, which many interpreted as a calculated insult. Gates was sufficiently angered to consider pulling down his whole program. After talking to Ambassador Jon Huntsman, Gates decided to proceed, to raise directly with Hu Jintao his concern about the timing of the J-20 flight, and to report to the media afterward on that aspect of his conversation. Hu seemed surprised when Gates spoke of the matter and questioned his colleagues down the line about it until an army officer explained to Hu that it was a coincidence. Whether this was true or not, Gates had made his point, while Hu seemed displeased by the J-20 distraction. The episode served as a reminder of the poor communication between China's military and the rest of its hierarchy, and the importance of a U.S.-China dialogue to try to bridge the gap.[6]

The Hu Visit

From the Chinese perspective, the visit was two-thirds of the way to being a success as soon as the welcoming ceremony was complete. It was an unseasonably warm and sunny January morning that unfolded without incident—no screaming disruptions from the press gallery (as had occurred during Hu's previous visit and Deng Xiaoping's visit in 1979), no misstatements of the name of China, no need for President Obama to yank Hu by the arm (as President Bush had) to move him in the right direction. After putting literally hundreds of hours into planning for the visit, the chief of protocol, Capricia Marshall, breathed an audible sigh of relief when the ceremony was over. Chinese media were able to broadcast the ceremony back to China without the need to explain or censor embarrassments, which was in their eyes an important statement of U.S. respect for China.

On the night before the welcoming ceremony, Obama hosted Hu for a small dinner in a White House ceremonial room, attended on the U.S. side only by Secretary Clinton and Tom Donilon. Obama used the dinner to try to drive to conclusion several of the unresolved issues.

He pressed Hu hard for language that would spell out what the Chinese had indicated privately, namely that they considered the North Korean uranium enrichment program a violation of the North's commitments and UN Security Council resolutions. The Chinese had thus far been unwilling to include such language in the joint statement they were negotiating with Kurt Campbell. Hu finally agreed to a formulation under which China would express "concern" over the North Korean program and oppose activities inconsistent with the 2005 joint statement and

North Korea's international obligations. It took several more calls between Campbell and me from midnight to 4 a.m. to finally squeeze acceptable language out of the Chinese negotiators. We regarded this as a significant step forward in putting China on record about the unacceptability of the uranium enrichment program, thereby undercutting North Korean attempts to extort further concessions in exchange for limiting or abandoning the program whenever negotiations resumed.[7]

Obama also sought to persuade Hu to agree to a proposal for senior-level talks involving both civilian officials and uniformed military officers on sensitive security issues, such as nuclear modernization, missile defense, outer space, cyberspace, and maritime security, which Jim Steinberg had first put on the table ten months earlier. Hu seemed skeptical since he was not sure how such talks would fit in with existing channels, but he promised to consider the matter further.

Obama and Hu went over familiar ground on economic issues. Hu did deliver news of China's decision to order 200 Boeing aircraft, which the administration had been pushing for in the preceding month, though precisely how these aircraft fit in with previous commitments was not immediately clear. For his part, Obama stressed that protecting human rights and democracy were central values of our system and foreign policy, and that China would be expected to heed universal standards in this regard. Hu replied, as he would at the joint press conference the next day, that China was making strides in this area but still had a long way to go.

The formal meetings in the Oval Office and the Cabinet Room the next day followed a predictable script and produced no major surprises. Americans recognized the development challenges facing China, the president said, and emphasized that he was not advocating reforms or changes that they thought would negatively affect China's growth. On the contrary, these ideas were consistent with China's move toward a more demand- and consumption-driven model. On security issues such as Iran, Sudan, and military-to-military relations, the two sides reaffirmed the progress they had made toward a more cooperative relationship.

The Chinese were very satisfied with the visit, particularly with the courtesy and bells and whistles surrounding it—the welcoming ceremony with a twenty-one-gun salute, the state dinner attended by two former presidents (Bill Clinton and Jimmy Carter), the business event with sixteen American and Chinese chief executive officers, the private dinner with the president, and the warm reception in Chicago the day after the Washington visit. Making the Chinese happy was not our principal objective, but it was a welcome outcome nonetheless. Given that Hu had to overcome internal opposition to the trip, especially at the end of a year marked by a number of squabbles between the two sides, it was important that he emerge with a greater sense of our commitment to the relationship.

Although the administration was not primarily seeking concrete deliverables, the visit had some good specific outcomes. Hu's criticism of North Korea was a significant step forward. Several days after Hu's visit, during another visit to Beijing by Jim Steinberg and me, the Chinese agreed to our proposal for a civilian-military senior dialogue on sensitive issues, which Hu had promised Obama he would consider further. He did, to good effect. The joint statement negotiated by Kurt Campbell was an impressive document, containing none of the hidden traps that might have disturbed allies and partners. In addition, the economic and trade agreements outlined in the previous month's meeting of the U.S.-China Joint Commission on Commerce and Trade, cochaired by Commerce Secretary Gary Locke, were codified by the visit.

But another lesson of the trip for me was the critical importance of properly shaping the public message surrounding such events. I understood that as a general matter, of course, but had felt badly burned by the negative media reaction to Obama's visit to China when I had seen the president perform superbly throughout. As I observed earlier, the public perception in that case had been shaped by an American media determined to portray the United States as a supplicant to a rising China to which it owed $1 trillion, while our less-than-stellar explanations of some of the public events (such as the Shanghai town hall meeting and the press conference) only served to feed the story. Although some excellent analyses had appeared—by Jim Fallows in *The Atlantic*, and several by John Pomfret in the *Washington Post* and Mark Landler in the *New York Times*—impressions had already been shaped.[8]

This time, the administration was determined not to allow a similar narrative to emerge unchallenged. As a first step, Secretary Geithner's speech shifted the focus of attention away from appreciation of the yuan as the sole measure of success, while Secretary Clinton in a major address on January 14 spoke of both the opportunities in the relationship and of the challenges, especially with respect to China's human rights shortcomings.[9]

President Obama also held two meetings in the week before the visit with outside experts, one with human rights and rule-of-law activists and one with leading China experts. Our team provided background briefings on the first meeting, demonstrating publicly the president's interest in these issues.[10]

The combination of good results and careful public messaging produced a visit that exceeded expectations and was well received in the United States. This outcome was in no way assured. Not only are major events in U.S.-China relations subject to intense scrutiny, but evaluations are often also based on completely unrealistic criteria, such as whether Washington persuaded Beijing to abandon long-standing practices and convictions, or whether it brought about systemic change to China's political system, or if, failing to do either, it was sufficiently aggressive, if not outright insulting, in criticizing China's shortcomings. It is not in President Obama's nature either to harbor unrealistic expectations or to browbeat or publicly humiliate guests. It also is not in his nature to have simple happy-talk conversations that fail to raise hard questions. The Obama I witnessed during the Hu trip was the same statesman I had seen in action throughout the previous two years. On this occasion, happily, the public assessments seemed to recognize that.

TWELVE

DEALING WITH
MULTIPLE DISASTERS IN JAPAN

FROM THE TIME I joined the Obama administration, I had planned to serve for about two years and then move on. National Security Council jobs are for the young, and I was already sixty-three when the Obama administration began. I felt that after two years of grinding work, it would be time to move aside for a fresh face. I also felt the need at some stage to increase my income potential, as thirty years of federal service had left me inadequately prepared for a satisfactory retirement. Much as I loved public service and felt not the slightest regret for the time spent in it, I knew that in 2011 I would cross a threshold and have to do something different. The successful completion of the Hu Jintao visit gave me a sense of satisfaction that the U.S.-China relationship was on a good trajectory, and the time had come to start thinking about a post-government future.

But before I could execute such a plan, one last crisis intervened. On March 11, 2011, I was awakened at 1:45 a.m. by a call from the White House Situation Room reporting that an earthquake measured at 8.9 on the Richter scale (subsequently raised to 9.0) had struck northeast Japan, and tsunami warnings had been issued. It took a few days for the scope of the disaster to become clear. Eventually, it became apparent that approximately 14,000 lives were lost, and another 13,000 were missing and presumed dead.

In the face of this natural disaster, unprecedented in modern Japanese history, the Obama administration immediately moved to set up a vigorous search and rescue and relief program to help the Japanese government save those who could be saved. We formed an interagency group, chaired at the Deputies Committee level by Denis McDonough and assisted by National Security Council director for resilience (disasters) Richard Reed and me, which concentrated at the outset on mobilizing relief efforts by U.S. Pacific Command (PACOM) and the U.S. Agency for International Development (USAID).

The PACOM-led relief efforts were organized with the characteristic brilliant efficiency of the U.S. military in disaster relief operations and provided indispensable support for remote and isolated towns cut off from normal services. Altogether, PACOM deployed some twenty-four ships, including the U.S.S. *Ronald Reagan* aircraft carrier, and 20,000 sailors, airmen, and marines to carry in food, tents, water, medicine, and other needed supplies and to fly out rescued civilians by helicopter. Their efforts saved lives and relieved hardship and were received with outspoken gratitude throughout Japan, demonstrating graphically one of the ways in which the alliance served ordinary Japanese.[1]

The assistance provided by the U.S. government in general and PACOM in particular went a long way toward solidifying public support in Japan for the relationship and alliance with the United States. The fraying caused by the mishaps of the Hatoyama period, and the difficulty in building a stable relationship when prime ministers had changed six times in five years, were all but forgotten in the wave of Japan's public appreciation for the U.S. response to the disaster, soon compounded by a nuclear meltdown. Japanese public support for the alliance was now greater and much more deeply embedded than before.

The relief operations generated few difficult policy decisions. Some who had worked with USAID on previous such operations in Haiti and other areas with weak local governance capabilities were accustomed to having the U.S. contingent essentially in charge. Danny Russel, Richard Reed, and I contended, however, that the Japanese authorities had substantial experience and demonstrated competence in organizing disaster relief, as they had shown after the Kobe earthquake of 1995. We noted that the Japanese welcomed financial support and the special mobilization and lift capabilities of PACOM, but not an on-the-ground task force seeking to substitute for their own government. After a few days, that argument was won, and USAID concentrated on providing resources rather than duplicating the Japanese government's capabilities.

NUCLEAR MELTDOWNS

Within a couple of days, however, it became apparent that the principal challenge to U.S. policymakers brought on by the disaster was the threat of multiple meltdowns at the nuclear reactor site at Fukushima, 160 miles northeast of Tokyo. Fukushima had six reactors, three of which were on line when the earthquake and tsunami struck. The other three were not, but their highly toxic fuel rods were stored in spent-fuel pools on site.

The reactors survived the earthquake apparently without fatal damage. But the tidal wave rose to forty-six feet, which was far greater than the five or six feet recorded for tsunamis earlier in the century. The disaster overwhelmed the electrical power running the reactor, back-up generators, and the grid servicing the whole region. Without power to the reactors and spent-fuel pools, it was impossible to cool either the active or spent fuel rods. In the absence of alternative cooling capacity, the water in the reactors and pools would inevitably boil off, leaving the rods exposed and triggering a partial or complete meltdown.

These developments posed huge risks that our interagency team attempted to evaluate. In assessing the situation, we were guided by John Holdren, the president's science adviser, who provided lucid and sound counsel at all hours of the day and night for the next five weeks. Other key actors in the massive interagency team were the deputy secretary of energy, Dan Poneman, and the chairman of the Nuclear Regulatory Commission, Greg Jaczko.

The interagency team struggled at the outset to obtain information about what was going on at Fukushima. Some believed the Japanese were not being entirely forthcoming with what they knew, trying to put an excessively optimistic gloss on the situation. Holdren, as well as staff at the Department of Energy (DOE), National Research Council (NRC), and NSC, was less critical. He pointed out that none of the instruments used to monitor developments inside the reactors were functional, so information was inevitably sketchy. Because of radiation leaks and hydrogen explosions, it was impossible to station utility staff on site for more than a few minutes at a time, so on-the-ground assessments were very difficult to come by. Besides, a small number of Japanese officials were facing multiple horrors of unimaginable scale, and to expect them to provide us with real-time accurate information seemed to me unrealistic. Although subsequent investigations have pointed to significant errors by the Japanese in estimating the threat and in putting out information in a timely way, the core problem was not a desire to cover up but rather the sheer difficulty of knowing what was going on at the reactor site.

The NRC and DOE dispatched experts to Tokyo who worked closely with the Japanese in evaluating possible solutions to the new challenges that arose daily. Holdren, Jaczko, and Poneman spoke regularly with old friends and counterparts in Japan, getting and sharing assessments. One day, the challenge was to cool reactor 2. The next day, it was reactor 3. The next day, it was a spent-fuel pool. Seawater was pumped into reactors to cool them. Then it was discovered that salt from the seawater was caking the fuel rods, making it even more difficult to cool them. It appeared that the radioactive steam had to be vented to prevent further hydrogen buildup and explosions, but that in turn heightened the fear of airborne radiation. Radioactive water in the bottom of the reactors was run off into the ocean to make the reactors accessible, but then radiation in the seawater rose to unacceptable levels. Each temporary solution seemed to generate a new problem, and each day that our interagency committee met, we seemed to be facing a new peril.

Our interagency team rapidly grew into the largest one in memory, as the radiation emanating from Fukushima sparked concerns over the safety of international aviation routes, the global food supply, the safety of the ocean, edibility of fish, and radioactive clouds sweeping across the Pacific. Every relevant agency became involved—the National Oceanic and Atmospheric Administration (NOAA), the Federal Drug Administration (FDA), the Environmental Protection Agency (EPA), Health and Human Services, Transportation, Interior, Justice, Customs, the Surgeon General, and Veterans Affairs, to name but a few that were relative strangers to the NSC process.

The agencies concerned with the potential impact on the U.S. homeland rapidly developed protocols to measure and mitigate the risks but found them to be minimal. Practices put in place included procedures for vetting food imports and cargo and passengers traveling from Japan to the United States. In addition, the EPA expanded its monitoring of radiation, detecting slightly elevated but harmless levels in several locations.

AMERICANS IN JAPAN

The principal challenge for the NSC chain of command was not the negligible threat to the U.S. homeland. Rather it was how to evaluate the risk for Americans—civilian and military—living in Japan and what to do about it.

Having served overseas in the State Department and having been responsible for the safety of American citizens in my jurisdiction when I served as an ambassador, I considered it the first responsibility of U.S. officials to protect the health, safety, and well-being of Americans overseas. This was not a concern to be weighed or balanced against others. It was an absolute priority.

But of course there is no such thing as absolute security. Whether one is facing foreign invasion, terrorism, civil unrest, ethnic warfare, poor health infrastructure, or a high crime rate, the safety of Americans is always at risk. Those responsible for their protection have to evaluate those risks and determine when they have become intolerable.

The Fukushima disaster was unique in this regard. The very thought of radiation can cause the public to panic in a way that other threats do not. Many Americans do not realize the degree to which they already are in fact exposed to radiation in their daily lives. It may be easy to evaluate and explain in a classroom the acceptability of slightly added risk associated with heightened exposure, but it becomes a far more difficult exercise when the audience consists of families with young children, which was the situation we faced in Japan.

Early in the crisis, we determined that we would apply EPA standards in making our recommendations in Japan. In other words, if a radiation level exceeded EPA standards and mitigating action or evacuation were recommended at that level in the United States, we would make the same recommendation to our citizens in Japan. While we did not want our recommendations to be out of sync with Japanese recommendations for their own population, we felt it would be a dereliction of responsibility to waive our own standards as an act of faith in an ally.

Above all else, what made reacting to the crisis so painfully difficult was the uncertainty surrounding the events in Fukushima, especially when it became evident that the Japanese government, or anyone else for that matter, did not have the ability to contain the crisis once electrical power was lost and the meltdowns began. For the first few weeks, the Japanese watched helplessly as the crisis spread from one reactor to the next. Little could be done to halt the multiple reactor breakdowns in the site's uniquely hostile environment. The engineering required to contain the problem would have been daunting under the best of circumstances. The environment at Fukushima was anything but benign.

In this atmosphere of high anxiety, inadequate information, and uncertain course of the catastrophes, we needed to make a succession of decisions with consequences for U.S. citizens in Japan, for U.S. relations with Japan, and for a longer-term presence in Japan. First, we had to decide whether to declare a larger evacuation zone around Fukushima than Japan did. Modeling conducted by the NRC and DOE indicated that an evacuation zone of fifty miles would be more consistent with U.S. radiation mitigation and evacuation standards than the Japanese zone of twenty kilometers, so the administration recommended that all U.S. citizens in the fifty-mile zone leave. Although there were almost no Americans in that area, the discrepancy between the Japanese and U.S. recommendations attracted unwelcome attention and subjected the Japanese government to some criticism. Of course it was considerably easier for us to err on the side of caution, since we had almost no Americans in the area and no responsibility to house or take care of them once they departed, whereas the Japanese had several million people there, all of them the government's responsibility if they moved.

Far more challenging, however, was the question of how to deal with the large American population in Tokyo and at the nearby U.S. bases in Yokota and Yokosuka: about 90,000 Americans lived in Tokyo alone, and there was a vital air force and navy presence at the two bases. Recommendations affecting those locations could send metaphorical shock waves throughout Japan.

The U.S. ambassador to Japan, John Roos, was under tremendous pressure from American government families in Tokyo to authorize their departure. The commander of U.S. Forces Japan was under comparable, arguably even greater pressure from dependents at the U.S. bases. The administration did not want to take such a step in the absence of a sound scientific reason for doing so. The White House science adviser offered no support for the claim of a radiation threat to Tokyo or the bases, although he could not at the outset provide long-term guarantees based on unknown contingencies. In fact, some foreign embassies in Tokyo had begun drawing down or moving facilities further south to Kyoto. We wanted to be sensitive to the needs and wishes of families but did not wish to trigger a panic in Tokyo.

A number of heated Deputies Committee meetings ensued at which both Ambassador Roos and military commanders strongly urged the government to authorize the departure of dependents. On March 16 Washington decided to authorize the voluntary departure of dependents, in essence telling U.S. official dependents that they were free to depart Japan at U.S. government expense but could not return until the voluntary departure order was terminated. All official personnel were ordered to remain in place. That decision helped to relieve the pressure building in the U.S. official community for more draconian action. The Japanese government reacted with relative equanimity, since the approval of voluntary departure did not imply judgments about Tokyo's safety.

But the relief was only temporary. The administration still lacked a solid basis for projecting future risk. Holdren and the DOE were working closely with Lawrence Livermore National Laboratory to try to develop a model for plausible worst-case scenarios, but it was taking time. In the absence of an authoritative model, other hypotheses filled the void and encouraged ill-considered decisions.

The Defense Department's Naval Nuclear Propulsion unit, which has responsibility for the nuclear power capabilities of the U.S. nuclear navy, has its own considerable expertise on nuclear issues. It serves as a sort of Defense in-house expert on nuclear subjects. It was natural that in this unique crisis, with so many navy equities at stake, its voice would have resonance.

Throughout March and April, the Naval Nuclear Propulsion unit offered extreme scenarios of the risks involved. Their assessments were invariably more alarmist than those offered by the NRC, DOE, and Holdren. As a result, in a number of instances Defense Department actions were inconsistent with those of the rest of the government.

When Washington announced the voluntary departure of civilian dependents from Tokyo, the Defense Department initially stated it was authorizing departure from the entire island of Honshu, not merely from the bases near Tokyo.[2] There was no good argument for that decision, and the agency backtracked within a day in the face of arguments from the rest of the interagency community.

In late March the Defense Department argued strongly for a decision to distribute iodine tablets to service members and dependents on an urgent basis as a prophylaxis against thyroid cancer caused by radioactive iodine. The administration of iodine is a controversial matter. To be effective, it must be administered at the right time and in the right dose, not at a random moment. It has significant side effects for many people. And it has limited effectiveness against thyroid cancer. Consequently, a decision to distribute tablets, much less take them, was not a simple matter. Nonetheless, the decision was made to authorize distribution of iodine tablets to official Americans and dependents. The embassy endeavored as well to make iodine tablets available to other American citizens living in Tokyo who requested them.[3]

In the wake of the decision to distribute iodine tablets, the Naval Nuclear Propulsion unit argued that radiation levels could under foreseeable circumstances soon exceed EPA standards at Yokosuka, which would have meant a considerably higher level in Tokyo. Obviously if that turned out to be true, we would need to issue directives to protect the health of American citizens, regardless of the Japanese assessment of the situation. Such directives, depending on how drastic they were, could either cause panic in Tokyo or a breach in the U.S.-Japan relationship. Danny Russel, Richard Reed, and I were determined that we not be stampeded into sudden action in the absence of a sound scientific basis, but we understood the urgent necessity of developing a sound analysis as a basis for a decision, whichever way it went.

I awakened Denis McDonough after midnight one night in late March describing the dilemma and the pressures we faced. He called John Holdren to ask him to provide the best model he could based on extreme scenarios at Fukushima so that we could see if our current precautions were adequate. Holdren did so immediately. The levels of radiation Holdren conveyed to us were utterly at odds with what the Naval Nuclear Propulsion unit had projected. Under plausible extreme scenarios, Holdren's model suggested that radioactivity at Yokosuka would be about 5 percent of what the Naval Nuclear Propulsion unit had projected. And only 1 or 2 percent of the radioactive particulate would be iodine, not most of it, as the Naval Nuclear Propulsion unit feared. Holdren's rapid and careful work had averted a potential slide toward unnecessary and damaging decisions.

But the pressure did not disappear. Because of the unpredictability of the situation at Fukushima, we needed to draw up contingency plans for the evacuation of all Americans from Tokyo and the bases in the event that the situation warranted it. That was normal and proper, although extremely unlikely. But once PACOM began planning for a noncombatant evacuation that theoretically could involve 90,000 people under conditions of panic, the information would inevitably leak and the process develop a certain momentum.

Predictably, the contingency planning leaked quickly. Stories ran in U.S. military media and the Japanese press that suggested evacuation was a real possibility.[4] I called the chief of naval operations, Admiral Gary Roughead, with whom I had had very good interactions in the past. I told him of my dismay at the way the story was percolating. I said that I was as strongly in favor of protecting American servicemen's health as anyone, but we needed a scientific basis for decisions. We also could not be casual about the future of the alliance by allowing a whimsical decisionmaking process to take hold.

Roughead understood my concerns and promised to correct the public messaging. Within an hour, he had called in the defense press and made unequivocal statements to the effect that our forces were not going anywhere, and that evacuation was not in the cards. Roughead's comments helped reverse a worrisome trend, and his statements were quickly echoed by other senior members of the chain of command, including PACOM Commander Admiral Willard.[5]

These daily crises in response to wildly speculative assessments and reports were testing our patience, not to mention our sleep cycles. We needed a firm scientific basis for decisions. Fortunately, Holdren and the DOE were about to produce one.

Working with Lawrence Livermore National Laboratory, Holdren developed a series of models based on plausible worst-case scenarios. They depicted simultaneous meltdowns at one or more reactors and complete drainage of the spent fuel pools at two reactors. The results for such worst-case scenarios, assuming unfavorable wind patterns from the reactor site and a lack of precipitation, suggested that radioactive plumes in excess of EPA standards would not reach within 75 to 100 miles of Tokyo, and we would have several days' notice before such a contingency could develop. In other words, there was no plausible scenario in which Tokyo, Yokosuka, or Yokota could be subject to dangerous levels of airborne radiation.

Armed with that information, Tom Donilon convened a Principals Committee meeting. Some at the meeting were still uneasy. They wondered to what degree the assessments were based on information, perhaps defective, supplied by the Japanese. Holdren replied that was not the case, and that they were based on models for these types of reactors provided by the NRC and General Electric, the manufacturer. That effectively settled the argument. From then on, there was no serious discussion of evacuation from Tokyo or the bases. Instead, we increased the flow of information to Americans on the ground about the situation and the risks in terms of airborne radiation and food and water contamination.

Although the Fukushima situation was far from stable, at least a scientific model was now in place to assess the risks to Americans. Washington shared the assessment with the Japanese government, as well as readings of ground radiation developed by U.S. experts brought into the theater. The risk of decisions with no basis in fact that could have undermined the alliance had been eliminated.

In crisis situations, drastic options with grave consequences inevitably have to be considered, as they were in this instance. However, the proper test of the process is whether such options are imprperly chosen, not whether they come up. In my view, the thorough and serious interagency processes, chaired respectively by Denis McDonough and Senior Director Richard Reed, did an excellent job of fully drawing out the facts, the scientific assessments, the considerable expertise of numerous agencies, and competing views. As a result, American citizens were fully informed and protected, while rash decisions were avoided. In this extremely complex set of challenges, with many unknowables and unknowns, the results vindicated the process.

THIRTEEN

LOOKING BACK, LOOKING AHEAD

U.S. FOREIGN POLICY often has been criticized for being too reactive and not strategic enough. The criticisms have come not only from the outside. I can't count the number of meetings I attended in which someone has declared emphatically, after several rounds of inconclusive argument, "We need a strategy."

In the real world, presidents and nations have no choice but to react to developments as they occur. Manifestos and road maps sound good in speeches, campaign documents, op-eds, and textbooks, but they rarely provide effective prescriptions for action when a fresh, unanticipated challenge arises. If they did, peace would long ago have been achieved in the Middle East. It is not the absence or inadequacy of road maps that has been the obstacle, but rather the intractability of the disputes and problems. A sound foreign policy requires the ability to manage complex disputes and immutable realities, so as to advance and protect American interests despite sometimes being unable to reshape those realities.

TACTICS AND STRATEGY

The National Security Council, the State Department, and the Department of Defense all regularly produce papers laying out global strategies and priorities.[1] Specialized offices produce these lengthy documents.

People around the bureaucracy review them. They are ceremoniously rolled out. When they are public documents, they are studiously read, and usually misinterpreted, at home and abroad. Then they are tucked away in safes and rarely referred to again, certainly not in times of crisis. In the face of yet one more demand for a strategy, one of my NSC colleagues said with exasperation and exaggeration, "In reality, there's no such thing as strategy. There are just a series of tactical decisions."

The daily work of the U.S. government's national security apparatus consists for the most part of making these tactical decisions. Insofar as a strategic vision is needed for many decisions, it is often not so much a fully developed, nuanced, and specific strategic plan but rather a thorough grounding in U.S. national interests. These interests do not change radically and quickly, and good foreign policy practitioners understand what they are. They are not based on Republican or Democratic, liberal or conservative principles. They are based on American principles. With the president's guidance and the support of the NSC's senior leadership, I tried hard to build a bipartisan consensus for our Asia policy based on this assumption, frequently calling in experts from both parties for discussions of our policy and welcoming criticism and comments. Such an inclusive process brought us ideas, and support, from all directions, not merely from predictable sources. One satisfying aspect of this process for me was that the extreme polarization that marked domestic politics in the Obama years was absent from foreign policy. While naturally there was criticism from Republicans and Congress, it was generally measured and not as intense as I have experienced in earlier administrations.

In this book I have spent a good deal of time describing the day-to-day decisionmaking that ultimately determines the success or failure of policy. We in the Obama NSC were not regularly reviewing national security strategies to make sure we were toeing a line. Rather, with U.S. national interest as our touchstone, we were trying to get positive outcomes for our country.

Indeed, many of the challenges our national security team faced were different from what we anticipated going into office, or they evolved from unexpected events. Every administration has to cope with surprises, and we did too. We were tested by North Korea's early belligerence and nuclear and missile tests, by Chinese assertiveness in maritime areas, by domestic politics in Japan and the disaster of March 2011, and by continuing economic weakness at home. The success or failure of an administration's foreign policy depends as much on how it responds to unanticipated developments as it does on strategic clarity at the outset.

Demands for strategic clarity can be overdone, but policy is not mere execution or tactics. Presidents do need overarching ideas and goals to shape the execution by their bureaucracies. The biggest foreign policy problems in fact require both strategy and tactics. Sometimes, different strategic perspectives will lead to significantly different policy decisions. Whether and how much to use American influence to secure democratic outcomes in the Arab world is a strategic decision, for example. Whether the United States should build a relationship marked primarily by cooperation with China or by confrontation is a strategic decision. How to pursue the objective of dismantling North Korea's nuclear program, whether primarily by pressure or by negotiations, requires strategic thinking about the U.S. presence in the region, its relations with allies, its relations with China, and its tolerance for risk. In chapter 1, I described the fundamental principles of the Obama administration's Asia-Pacific strategy, notably:

—Devote a higher priority to the Asia-Pacific region.

—React in a balanced way to the rise of China.

—Strengthen alliances and develop new partnerships.

—Expand the overall U.S. presence in the western Pacific and maintain its forward regional deployment.

—Understand that it is impossible to pursue a sound policy without economic recovery at home.

—Break the cycle of North Korean extortion and U.S. reward for bad behavior and freeze, degrade, and ultimately dismantle North Korea's nuclear weapons program.

—Join regional institutions that the United States has stayed apart from.

—Speak and act with clarity on the universality of human rights while understanding and taking into account the differences between societies.

The decisions President Obama made and the steps we took reflected these guiding principles. They may not have been in evidence every day, but their impact can be seen in the most important decisions we made and how we executed them. Among them, I highlight a few below.

Relationship with China. The administration endeavored to build a stable, predictable, and positive relationship with China, with substantial cooperation on political and security issues, progress on economic issues, and clarity on human rights issues. This entailed frequent and respectful interaction between Obama and top Chinese leaders, extensive strategic dialogue on the administration's perception of U.S. interests, the possible impact of unexpected developments, and firmness when the Chinese appeared to be overreaching, or allies needed to be reassured.

Freedom of the seas. We reaffirmed U.S. determination to ensure freedom of the seas and allow the U.S. Navy to operate effectively through deployments in the South China Sea, Yellow Sea, and East China Sea. Diplomatic support was also marshaled for our position in the South China Sea, particularly at the ASEAN Regional Forum in 2010.

North Korea. Bilateral and multilateral sanctions against North Korea were ratcheted up. We also refused to resume talks for the sake of talks, and we redefined the basis for serious negotiations.

South Korea. The administration strongly supported South Korea militarily and diplomatically in response to North Korean provocations and aggression by conducting a series of joint military exercises, which included deploying an aircraft carrier to the Yellow Sea, leading an investigation and response to the sinking of the *Cheonan*, and giving special prominence and attention to President Lee Myung-bak of South Korea. Through these steps and completion of negotiation of the U.S.-South Korea Free Trade Agreement, we arguably brought the relationship with the South to its strongest level in recent memory.

U.S.-Japan alliance. We stood firm for the enduring interests of and necessary military facilities for the U.S.-Japan alliance at a time when Japanese leaders were questioning them, but we did so without polarizing the two sides or rallying Japanese public opinion against us. Instead, the alliance emerged not only reaffirmed but also more soundly based on support from both of Japan's major political parties.

Response to disaster. The administration provided every possible support for Japan and its people in response to the earthquake, tsunami, and nuclear meltdown and ensured that our actions and decisions to protect American lives did not undercut the U.S.-Japan alliance.

Tripartite cooperation. Cooperation between the United States and its key Northeast Asian allies, Japan and South Korea, was fostered through much greater consultation and policy coordination pertaining to North Korea and through a trilateral foreign ministers' meeting hosted by Secretary Clinton.

East Asia Summit. By joining the East Asia Summit and beating back proposals for regional integration that would have excluded the United States, we laid the basis for U.S. leadership in the new emerging regional architecture of the Asia-Pacific region and demonstrated graphically the higher priority the Obama administration placed on the Asia-Pacific.

Relations with ASEAN. The Obama administration acceded to the ASEAN Treaty of Amity and Cooperation; held two presidential meetings with the ten ASEAN leaders; stationed a U.S. ambassador to ASEAN in Jakarta; built a relationship with Indonesia through the establishment of a comprehensive partnership, a presidential visit to Indonesia, and restoration of relations with the Indonesian military's counterterrorism unit; and initiated a diplomatic dialogue with Burma that has helped encourage political reform and the beginnings of an end to Burma's isolation.

Trade. We completed negotiations on the U.S.-Korea free trade agreement and launched negotiations on a Trans-Pacific Partnership trade agreement.

We felt that our policy actions reinforced America's presence and influence in Asia. More important than our own judgment, the states of the region were overwhelmingly positive in their reaction to our policy.[2]

WHAT'S NEXT?

I left the administration in April 2011 believing that the policies we had pursued and the steps we had taken had enhanced U.S. influence and prestige in the Asia-Pacific region. But of course some of the key issues still had to play out. There were no quick fixes to problems like North Korea's nuclear program, or answers to questions like the ultimate impact of China's rise.

The fluctuations and frictions in the U.S.-China relationship transfixed the media, which ran numerous articles citing growing tensions. But this is a seriously flawed way to view the forward movement in the U.S.-China relationship. Frictions are bound to arise in the relationship between the world's dominant power and its major rising power when their histories, cultures, interests, and values are vastly different. This is only to be expected, unless one side completely subordinates itself to the other. That will not happen. So a relationship with a certain amount of turbulence and disagreement should be seen as inevitable and natural. The test of success lies not in avoiding such turbulence and disagreement, but in our managing it so as to promote U.S. national and global interests.

The relationship will face large challenges. The potentially most perilous concerns Taiwan. The United States insists on a peaceful resolution of differences between the People's Republic of China and Taiwan, whereas China insists on the unbreakable unity of the Chinese nation. Right now, cross-strait relations are on a good track. They should not be disrupted by American gratuitous insults to Beijing or American abandonment of Taipei. This is of course easier said than done and will be tested primarily by decisions on arms sales in the short run.

Some challenges will arise in the economic realm. The most important step in addressing them is to get our own house in order in the wake of the financial meltdown and recession of 2008. Until that happens, many Americans will consider China a source of problems, rather than a boon to their economic well-being, and will be tempted to sink into protectionism. But that will not help promote economic recovery. Rather, it will harm America's broader international interests. This is an issue that cannot be addressed satisfactorily without the help of a China that is willing to assume responsibility for the international impact of its actions, whether with respect to currency, industrial policy, or other economic concerns. A China that focuses narrowly on its own interests will not be a stable economic partner for the United States.

In the realm of international security, the United States will want active Chinese cooperation on some issues, like Iran and North Korea. On others, like the evolving reform of the Arab world, it will want China to do no harm. Afghanistan and Pakistan fall somewhere in between. It is certainly in China's interest to see a stable, secular, and developing Pakistan and Afghanistan, but Beijing is so programmed to see India as a rival in the region and the United States as a potential rival that comprehensive coordination of policy is likely to be a bridge too far. Cooperation on all of these issues will greatly depend on the overall state of the U.S.-China relationship. If China considers the United States a strategic threat, that will color its approach in each case. If, on the other hand, it thinks the

United States plays a relatively benign role in their international security, its cooperation will come more easily.

Trying to predict with precision what China will look like a generation or even a decade from now is a daunting task for Chinese as much as for American observers. The most consequential geopolitical events of the past two decades—the collapse of the Soviet Union and its empire, the attack on the World Trade Center and the Pentagon, the Arab Spring, the global financial meltdown of 2008—were foreseen by very few. That can also be said of China's opening in the 1970s and the Tiananmen crisis of 1989.

Although it is impossible to predict cataclysmic events of that nature with confidence, certain broad trends likely to shape events are discernible. In China's case, it appears that a collapse in the style of the Soviet Union, one that marginalizes China from global affairs, is an extremely unlikely event. In the past three decades China has changed in ways that the Soviet Union never did. Its economic growth has created institutions, habits, capabilities, and expectations among its people that should limit the impact of future crises, no matter how pervasive. Although ethnic strife of the kind that undermined the Soviet Union does exist in China, it is much less prevalent.

China's system of one-party rule, exclusion of the broad population from political decisionmaking, continuing severe constraints on freedom of expression, and slow movement toward the rule of law may be sustainable for some time, as long as the leadership can successfully promote economic growth and manage the problems flowing from economic transformation. But they cannot be sustained indefinitely unless China truly is unique among successful nations in the twenty-first century. Other societies have come to recognize, sometimes through foresight and evolution, sometimes through revolution, that populations expect to play an active role in their governance. There are mounting frictions in China over inequalities in wealth, corruption, lack of transparency in decisionmaking, the treatment of hundreds of millions of migrant workers, and unemployment, to name but a few of the challenges. The 500 million Chinese surfing the Internet know much more about China's problems than their parents did, even if they have experienced them far less. This is likely to mean that China's governance system will change, perhaps significantly, in the years to come. Indeed Premier Wen Jiabao has said as much.

This does not mean that the Chinese system will soon be democratic, or resemble the American one, but it is likely to be different than it is now, notwithstanding the impressive adaptability that the Chinese Communist Party has demonstrated over the past three decades. The overall trend in China since the 1970s, despite short-term setbacks and repression, has been toward a more pluralistic and open system. That overall trend is likely to continue, with a more open and pluralistic system a decade from now.

China can become America's global adversary, but that is neither a predetermined outcome nor, in my opinion, the most likely one. In the past century the United States has come into conflict not with rising powers per se, but with rising powers that have had imperial ambitions, namely, Germany, Japan, and the Soviet Union. China at present has limited demands with the potential to trigger a conflict with its neighbors or with the United States: Taiwan, for example, and some maritime claims that are very unlikely to lead to large-scale hostilities. For China to directly challenge America's security interests, it would have to acquire ambitions and habits that it does not at present display. The United States should not behave in a way that encourages the Chinese to move in that direction.

As strong as China appears from the outside, it presents a very different face to its own leaders and people. With a per capita income only 10 to 15 percent of that in the United States and 700 million people still living in the countryside, China is a unique hybrid: the world's second largest economy with a substantial impact on the global system but fundamentally still a developing country. Indeed, its per capita income ranks ninety-first on the International Monetary Fund's global listing and hundredth on the World Bank's. In all likelihood, the next generation of China's leaders will understand that their principal challenge lies in improving that ranking, not in undertaking foreign adventures. This is not an assured outcome, nor one that outsiders can control, but Washington can help shape China's decisions by pursuing a policy that welcomes its continued growth, maintains U.S. strength in the region, and demonstrates that Americans are prepared to live with not only a poor China but also a strong and prosperous one that abides by global rules.

U.S. foreign policy also must step up to the other challenges in the region. Those emerging from Japan, for example, are greater than at any time since the 1980s. It appears the United States will have to deal with a succession of weak, short-term cabinets there. The Democratic Party of Japan has been severely damaged, and the Liberal Democratic Party has not revived. That, on top of the task of recovery from the earthquake, tsunami, and nuclear meltdowns, probably means a more inward-looking Japan. The Okinawa basing issues, while framed by an umbrella agreement supported by both governments, are not resolved. That agreement could still come undone. More fundamental questions remain about the long-term sustainability of 48,000 U.S. military personnel sixty-six years after the end of World War II. Politics in Japan and budget problems in the United States may force Washington to decide whether a more modest military presence could still adequately serve U.S. interests without causing anxieties about U.S. staying power. There is certainly nothing magical about the current troop deployment level. As long as Washington embarks on a serious dialogue about future commitments, future requirements, and future missions, adjustments should not prove excessively disruptive.

The challenges arising out of North Korea are somewhat more daunting. The next several years will tell whether there is a peaceful route to the North's denuclearization, whether there are circumstances under which North Korea's nuclear program can be eliminated. If not, the United States will have to adjust its security strategy to deal with a possible nuclear threat to its homeland and its allies from an unstable rogue state. It will be a great surprise if this issue can be resolved in the remainder of an Obama administration. A freeze and a rollback would seem like a plausible medium-term objective. The test will be whether the Obama administration is able to orchestrate a resumption of direct negotiation and Six-Party Talks and through them press for a freeze and rollback that includes the North's uranium enrichment program. The best-thought-out plans will not work if North Korea remains intransigent.

The death of North Korean leader Kim Jong-il in December 2011, and the succession of his young and inexperienced son, Kim Jong-un, introduces new uncertainties about North Korea's future. There is nothing known about Kim Jong-un's background that provides a basis for confidence that he will be a closet reformer, nor have the decisiveness to break out of his country's isolation by negotiating an end to its nuclear program. His ability to maintain himself in power and keep the decrepit North Korean regime afloat is far from assured. The bottom line is that the Korean peninsula is entering a new period of heightened unpredictability, which is likely to make a negotiated end to North Korea's nuclear program even harder to achieve.

Developments in Southeast Asia may be locally unsettling but should not have an adverse effect on U.S. interests. However, the United States must be prepared to deal with a dynamic in Thailand and the Philippines dominated by disputes between the rich and the poor, the elites and the common people, and urban and rural populations. Populist strongmen have alternated with representatives of the mainstream elite, the common denominator being a high degree of corruption. Without fundamental economic and social reform, it will be hard to escape this dynamic. Indonesia and Malaysia have some of the same challenges related to corruption, but they have been able to put in place political systems and parties that have the potential to produce stable growth in a politically peaceful environment. Singapore appears to be evolving toward a more competitive, pluralistic system, with minimal risk to the basic economic and social structures that have made it an international success story. There are preliminary indications that the administration's diplomatic engagement with Burma has helped to encourage some political thaw there, with greater space for democracy leader Aung San Suu Kyi to play an active public role, but the road to that end remains a long one.

To deal with these various developments, the president of the United States will need to pursue a strategy that addresses the issues outlined here, as well as devote sufficient time, energy, and resources to achieving it. The greatest task will be to forge a policy that is not premised on inevitable mutual hostility with China, nor on the notion that China's better angels will determine its future. The goal should be to build trust and ties with China, and not see such efforts as appeasement or unacceptable accommodation. China and the United States are ultimately likely to see each other in similar ways, either primarily as hostile or as benign; it is unlikely that the two will see each other profoundly differently. Just as Americans believe their strength does not mean that they are inherently aggressive or dangerous to world peace, China is capable of choosing to restrain its future military strength as well.

While one can hope for these positive outcomes and work with the Chinese to try to achieve them, it is essential to be prepared for other contingencies. Thus the United States needs to maintain its forward deployment, superior military forces and technological edge, its economic strength and engagement with the region, its alliances, and its enhanced relationships with other emerging powers. Chinese analysts are likely to consider all these traits to be hostile to China, just as every Chinese political and military advance, such as the development of an aircraft carrier, will be depicted as a threat to America.

Future presidents will need to find the right balance in China policy, so as to maintain America's strength and watchfulness but not fall into the classic security dilemma, wherein each side believes that growing capabilities reflect hostile intent and responds by producing that reality. I believe that President Obama struck that balance. I felt honored to be part of his administration in trying to achieve it.

US. and China must not Fall into the classic
Security dilemma whereaach side believes that
growing capabilities reflect hostile intent and responds
by producing that reality

NOTES

NOTES TO THE PROLOGUE

1. Barack Obama, Commencement Address, Knox College, Galesburg, Ill., June 4, 2005 (http://departments.knox.edu/newsarchive/news_events/2005/obama address.html).

2. John Heilemann and Mark Halperin, *Game Change: Obama and the Clintons, McCain and Palin, and the Race of a Lifetime* (New York: Harper, 2010).

3. Mike Chinoy, *Meltdown: The Inside Story of the North Korean Nuclear Crisis* (New York: St. Martin's Press, 2008).

4. For insights into presidential transitions and how key players involved saw the challenges, see Kurt M. Campbell and James B. Steinberg, *Difficult Transitions* (Brookings, 2008).

NOTES TO CHAPTER ONE

1. The ASEAN Regional Forum, established in 1993, is a multilateral institution centered on the Association of Southeast Asian Nations (ASEAN) and consists of twenty-seven countries that meet annually to discuss regional security issues at the foreign-minister level.

2. Amit Baruah, "A New APEC Agenda," *Frontline* (India), vol. 18 (November 10–23, 2001) (www.hindu.com/fline/fl1823/18230580.htm); Gary LaMoshi, "APEC Terrorized Out of Focus," *Asia Times,* October 31, 2002 (www.atimes. com/atimes/Asian_Economy/DJ31Dk01.html).

3. Favorable views of the United States in Indonesia in 2003 were 15 percent. See Pew Research Center, *Pew Global Attitudes Survey,* June 12, 2008 (http://pew global.org/files/pdf/260.pdf).

4. Richard M. Nixon, "Asia after Viet Nam," *Foreign Affairs,* October 1967 (www.foreignaffairs.com/articles/23927/richard-m-nixon/asia-after-viet-nam).

5. Aaron L. Friedberg, *A Contest for Supremacy: China, America and the Struggle for Mastery in Asia* (New York: W. W. Norton, 2011); Gideon Rachman, "Containing China," *Washington Quarterly* 19, no. 1 (1996); Henry A. Kissinger, "China Containment Won't Work," *Washington Post*, June 13, 2005; Henry Kissinger, *On China* (New York: Penguin Press, 2011).

6. This observation is based on conversations with several officials who served in the Bush White House and State Department.

7. Glen S. Fukushima, "Why Japan Prefers Bush," *Japan Times*, September 9, 2004 (http://search.japantimes.co.jp/cgi-bin/eo20040909a1.html).

8. Henry Kissinger, *Diplomacy* (New York: Simon and Schuster, 1995).

NOTES TO CHAPTER TWO

1. The Six-Party Talks were a dialogue mechanism established in 2003 during the Bush administration and designed to address the denuclearization of North Korea. The participants were China, Japan, North and South Korea, Russia, and the United States.

2. On Hillary Clinton's speech to 2,000 students at Ewha Womans University, see Kang In-sun, "How Clinton Stole Korean Hearts," *Chosun Ilbo*, February 25, 2009 (http://english.chosun.com/site/data/html_dir/2009/02/25/200902256 1014.html).

3. "Gist of Clinton's Talks with Nakasone," Kyodo News Agency, February 17, 2009 (accessed August 5, 2011, via BBC Worldwide Monitoring on Nexis).

4. Michael Green and Nicholas Szechenyi, "U.S.-Japan Relations: A Fresh Start," *Comparative Connections* 11 (April 2009): 15–23. Subsequently, Ozawa referred to Americans as "simple-minded" and voiced strong opposition to the U.S. presence in Afghanistan.

5. Kang In-sun, "How Clinton Stole Korean Hearts," *Chosun Ilbo*, February 25, 2009 (http://english.chosun.com/site/data/html_dir/2009/02/25/200902256 1014.html); "South Korean President Calls for More Cooperation with U.S. on North Korea," Yonhap News Agency, February 20, 2009 (accessed August 5, 2011, via BBC Worldwide Monitoring on Nexis).

6. Mike Chinoy, *Meltdown: The Inside Story of the North Korean Nuclear Crisis* (New York: St. Martin's Press, 2008).

7. Mark Landler, "Clinton Paints China Policy with a Green Hue," *New York Times*, February 21, 2009 (www.nytimes.com/2009/02/22/world/asia/22diplo.html).

8. "Clinton: Chinese Human Rights Can't Interfere with Other Crises," CNN, February 21, 2009 (http://articles.cnn.com/2009-02-21/politics/clinton. china. asia_1_human-rights-china-policy-chinese-president-hu-jintao?_s=PM: POLITICS).

9. Glenn Kessler, "Clinton Criticized for Not Trying to Force China's Hand: Advocacy Groups Urge Her to Put Human Rights Front and Center," *Washington Post*, February 21, 2009 (www.washingtonpost.com/wp-dyn/content/article/2009/02/20/AR2009022000967_pf.html).

10. Glenn Kessler, "Experts Divided over Whether Clinton Should Push China on Human Rights," *Washington Post*, February 23, 2009 (www.washingtonpost.com/wp-dyn/content/article/2009/02/22/AR 2009022200867.html).

NOTES TO CHAPTER THREE

1. James Mann, *About Face: A History of America's Curious Relationship with China, from Nixon to Clinton* (New York: Vintage, 2000); Patrick Tyler, *A Great Wall: Six Presidents and China* (New York: Public Affairs, 1999).

2. Alan D. Romberg, *Rein In at the Brink of Precipice: American Policy toward Taiwan and U.S.-PRC Relations* (Washington: Henry L. Stimson Center, 2003).

3. In a joint statement issued at the time of President Jiang Zemin's 1997 visit to Washington, the two sides agreed, "The two Presidents are determined *to build toward* a constructive strategic partnership between the United States and China . . . [and] to achieve this goal, they agree to approach U.S.-China relations from a long-term perspective."

4. Jesse Lee, "The President Meets with Chinese Foreign Minister Yang Jiechi," *The White House Blog*, March 12, 2009 (www.whitehouse.gov/blog/2009/03/12/president-meets-with-chinese-foreign-minister-yang-jiechi-0).

5. White House, Office of the Press Secretary, "Statement on Bilateral Meeting with President Hu of China," April 1, 2009 (www.whitehouse.gov/the_press_office/Statement-On-Bilateral-Meeting-With-President-Hu-Of-China/); "Chinese, U.S. Presidents Meet in London on Important Issues," Xinhua News Agency, April 1, 2009 (http://news. xinhuanet.com/english/2009-04/01/content_11115747.htm).

6. Michael D. Shear, "Obama Picks Huntsman, Republican Governor of Utah, as Ambassador to China," *Washington Post*, May 17, 2009 (www.washingtonpost.com/wp-dyn/content/article/2009/05/16/AR2009051600917.html).

7. McKay Coppins, "The Manchurian Candidate," *Newsweek*, January 1, 2011 (www.newsweek.com/2011/01/04/the-manchurian-candidate.html).

NOTES TO CHAPTER FOUR

1. Jonathan D. Pollack, *No Exit: North Korea, Nuclear Weapons and International Security* (London: International Institute for Strategic Studies, 2011).

2. Council on Foreign Relations, "Presidential Debate Transcript, Mississippi," Essential Documents, September 26, 2008 (www.cfr.org/us-election-2008/presidential-debate-transcript-mississippi/p17380); "President Barack Obama's

Inaugural Address," *The White House Blog*, January 21, 2009 (www.whitehouse.gov/blog/inaugural-address/).

3. I attributed this disconnect not to disagreements with Secretary Clinton, but to the momentum of the bureaucracy in the absence of intervening political leadership reflecting the new administration. Deputy Secretary Steinberg and the assistant secretary of state for East Asian and Pacific affairs were not yet confirmed by the Senate or in place.

4. Blaine Harden, "North Korean Missile Test a Growing Possibility," *Washington Post*, March 27, 2009 (www.washingtonpost.com/wp-dyn/content/article/2009/03/26/AR2009032600414.html); "S. Korea Says Rocket Launch by North Threat to Regional Security," Yonhap News Agency, March 26, 2009 (accessed August 5, 2011, via BBC Worldwide Monitoring on Nexis).

5. "Japan—Editorials Call Draft UNSC Resolution 'Stricter,' Stress China's Role," Open Source Center Report, June 12, 2009 (accessed August 5, 2011, via World News Connection).

6. Choe Sang-hun, "N. Korea Issues Threat on Uranium," *New York Times*, April 29, 2009 (www.nytimes.com/2009/04/30/world/asia/30korea.html).

7. Elisabeth Bumiller, "North Korea Is Warned by Gates on Testing," *New York Times*, May 29, 2009 (www.nytimes.com/2009/05/30/world/asia/30military.html).

8. Choe Sang-hun, "In South Korea, Freed U.S. Journalists Come under Harsh Criticism," *New York Times*, August 21, 2009 (www.nytimes.com/2009/08/22/world/asia/22journalists.html).

9. "N. Korea Frees U.S. Reporters after Bill Clinton Visit," *Chosun Ilbo*, August 5, 2009 (http://english.chosun.com/site/data/html_dir/2009/08/05/2009080500260.html); Glenn Kessler, "During Visit by Bill Clinton, North Korea Releases American Journalists," *Washington Post*, August 5, 2009 (www.washingtonpost.com/wp-dyn/content/article/2009/08/04/AR2009080400684.html).

10. United Nations Security Council, Department of Public Information, "Security Council, Acting Unanimously, Condemns in Strongest Terms Democratic People's Republic of Korea Nuclear Test, Toughens Sanctions," June 12, 2009 (www.un.org/News/Press/docs/2009/sc9679.doc.htm).

11. Choe Sang-hun, "South Korea Says Freighter from North Turns Back," *New York Times*, July 6, 2009 (www.nytimes.com/2009/07/07/world/asia/07korea.html); Ian MacKinnon and James Fontanella-Khan, "N. Korean Weapons 'Were Bound for Middle East,'" *Financial Times*, December 14, 2009 (www.ft.com/intl/cms/s/0/40 d1f000-e7bc-11de-8a02-00144feab49a,s01=1.html#axzz1STmNzzby); "UAE 'Seizes N. Korea Arms Cargo,'" BBC, August 28, 2009 (http://news.bbc.co.uk/2/hi/asia-pacific/8227991.stm).

Notes to Chapter Five

1. Yasuke Murayama and Hiroshi Ito, "China Policy Architects to Leave Obama Administration," *Asahi Shimbun*, April 16, 2011 (www.asahi.com/english/TKY201104150141.html/).

2. "Hatoyama, Obama Hold First Meeting," *Japan Times*, September 25, 2009 (http://search.japantimes.co.jp/cgi-bin/nn20090925a4.html).

3. "Japanese Ruling Party's Ozawa Arrives in China," Kyodo News Agency, December 10, 2009 (accessed August 5, 2011, via BBC Worldwide Monitoring on Nexis); "Ruling Parties of China, Japan Agree on Seeking Stronger Overall Relationship," Xinhua News Agency, December 10, 2009 (http://news.xinhuanet.com/english/2009-12/10/content_12626887.htm).

4. "U.S.' Gates Calls for Japan to Implement Forces Realignment Plan," Kyodo News Agency, October 20, 2009 (accessed July 18, 2011, via BBC Worldwide Monitoring on Nexis).

5. White House, Office of the Press Secretary, "Remarks by President Obama at Suntory Hall," November 14, 2009 (www.whitehouse.gov/the-press-office/remarks-president-barack-obama-suntory-hall), and "Remarks by President Barack Obama and Prime Minister Yukio Hatoyama of Japan in Joint Press Conference," November 13, 2009 (www.whitehouse.gov/the-press-office/remarks-president-barack-obama-and-prime-minister-yukio-hatoyama-japan-joint-press).

6. "U.S. President Queries Japan PM on Ability to 'Follow Through' on Base Issue," Kyodo News Agency, April 18, 2010 (accessed August 5, 2011, via BBC Worldwide Monitoring on Nexis).

7. Daniel Sneider, "Did Washington Bring Down the Japanese Prime Minister?" *Slate*, June 3, 2010 (www.slate.com/id/2255924/).

Notes to Chapter Six

1. Tsering Shakya, *The Dragon in the Land of Snows: A History of Modern Tibet since 1947* (New York: Penguin, 2000); Melvyn C. Goldstein, *The Snow Lion and the Dragon: China, Tibet, and the Dalai Lama* (University of California Press, 1999).

2. Office of His Holiness the Dalai Lama, "President Barack Obama's Emissary Calls on HH the Dalai Lama," September 14, 2009 (www.dalailama.com/news/post/392-president-barack-obamas-emissary-calls-on-hh-the-dalai-lama).

3. John Pomfret, "Obama's Meeting with the Dalai Lama Is Delayed," *Washington Post*, October 5, 2009 (www.washingtonpost.com/wp-dyn/content/article/2009/10/04/AR2009100403262.html).

4. "No Time for the Dalai Lama," *Wall Street Journal*, October 6, 2009 (http://online.wsj.com/article/SB10001424052748704471504574449420327844600.html); "Obama Bows Again," *Washington Times*, October 6, 2009 (www.washingtontimes.com/news/2009/oct/6/obama-bows-again/).

5. White House, Office of the Press Secretary, "Background Briefing by a Senior Administration Official on the President's Meeting with President Hu of China," September 22, 2009 (www.whitehouse.gov/the-press-office/background-briefing-a-senior-administration-official-presidents-meeting-with-presid); David E. Sanger, "Security Council Adopts Nuclear Arms Measure," *New York Times*, September 24, 2009 (www.nytimes.com/2009/09/25/world/25prexy.html).

6. John Pomfret and Joby Warrick, "China's Backing on Iran Followed Dire Predictions," *Washington Post*, November 26, 2009 (/www.washingtonpost.com/wp-dyn/content/article/2009/11/25/AR2009112504112.html).

7. Morton Abramowitz, "Obama Goes to China," *National Interest*, December 2, 2009 (http://nationalinterest.org/article/obama-goes-to-china-3319).

8. Saibal Dasgupta and Indrani Bagchi, "Obama Okay with Beijing Monitoring Indo-Pak Ties?" *Times of India*, November 18, 2009 (http://articles.timesofindia.indiatimes.com/2009-11-18/india/28069128_1_joint-statement-india-and-pakistan-obama-s-china).

9. White House, Office of the Press Secretary, "Remarks by President Obama at Town Hall Forum with Future Chinese Leaders," November 16, 2009 (www.whitehouse.gov/the-press-office/remarks-president-barack-obama-town-hall-meeting-with-future-chinese-leaders).

10. Ronald Reagan, "Remarks at Fudan University in Shanghai, China (April 30, 1984)," Ronald Reagan Presidential Library (www.reagan.utexas.edu/archives/speeches/1984/43084e.htm [July 19, 2011]).

11. Helene Cooper and David Barboza, "Obama Wades into Internet Censorship in China Address," *New York Times*, November 16, 2009 (www.nytimes.com/2009/11/17/world/asia/17shanghai.html).

12. Jeremy Goldkorn, "The Case of the Missing Obama Front Page," Danwei Website, November 19, 2009 (www.danwei.org/front_page_of_the_day/the_case_of_the_missing_obama.php).

13. "Cap and trade" is a system used in Europe that issues permits to companies to emit carbon up to a certain limit and compels them to buy additional permits on the open market if they exceed that limit, or "cap."

14. William Antholis and Strobe Talbott, *Fast Forward: Ethics and Politics in the Age of Global Warming* (Brookings, 2010).

NOTES TO CHAPTER SEVEN

1. In his speech opening the U.S.-China first Strategic and Economic Dialogue on July 27, 2009, President Obama said among other things: "Some in China think that America will try to contain China's ambitions; some in America think that there is something to fear in a rising China. I take a different view. And I believe President Hu takes a different view, as well. I believe in a future where China is a strong, prosperous and successful member of the community of nations; a future

when our nations are partners out of necessity, but also out of opportunity. This future is not fixed, but it is a destination that can be reached if we pursue a sustained dialogue like the one that you will commence today, and act on what we hear and what we learn."

2. The Obama administration announced in December 2009 its intention to negotiate a free trade agreement called the Trans-Pacific Partnership with eight other countries: Australia, New Zealand, Singapore, Peru, Chile, Malaysia, Vietnam, and Brunei.

3. Keith Bradsher, "U.S. Deal with Taiwan Has China Retaliating," *New York Times*, July 20, 2011 (www.nytimes.com/2010/01/31/world/asia/31china.html).

4. Michael Bristow, "Envoys of Tibet's Dalai Lama in New China Talks," BBC, January 26, 2010 (http://news.bbc.co.uk/2/hi/8480022.stm).

5. "White House Sends the Dalai Lama out the Back Door with the Trash," *Rush Limbaugh Show*, February 19, 2010 (www.rushlimbaugh.com/home/daily/site_021910/content/01125108.guest.html).

6. Edward Wong, "Chinese Military Seeks to Extend Its Naval Power," *New York Times*, April 23, 2010 (www.nytimes.com/2010/04/24/world/asia/24navy.html).

7. White House, Office of the Press Secretary, "Statement by Press Secretary Robert Gibbs on China," March 29, 2010 (www.whitehouse.gov/the-press-office/statement-press-secretary-robert-gibbs-china); U.S. Department of State, "The Deputy Secretary's Trip to the Balkans and Asia," FPC Briefing, March 29, 2010 (http://fpc.state.gov/139203.htm).

8. U.S. Department of the Treasury, Press Center, "Statement of Treasury Secretary Geithner on the Report to Congress on International Economic and Exchange Rate Policies," April 3, 2010 (www.treasury.gov/press-center/press-releases/pages/tg627.aspx).

9. David E. Sanger and Mark Landler, "China Pledges to Work with U.S. on Iran Sanctions," *New York Times*, April 12, 2010 (www.nytimes.com/2010/04/13/world/13summit.html).

10. Michael Wines, "China Blames U.S. for Strained Relations," *New York Times*, March 7, 2010 (www.nytimes.com/2010/03/08/world/asia/08china.html); Geoff Dyer, "China: Relations with U.S. Come under New Strain," *Financial Times*, January 26, 2010 (www.ft.com/intl/cms/s/0/90ea18d8-0945-11df-ba88-00144feabdc0.html#axzz1SgLbRdtY).

11. David Shambaugh, "The Year China Showed Its Claws," *Financial Times*, February 16, 2010 (www.ft.com/intl/cms/s/0/7503a600-1b30-11df-953f-00144feab49a.html#axzz1T8u3wnXy); Michael D. Swaine, "Perceptions of an Assertive China," *China Leadership Monitor*, no. 32. Spring 2010 (http://media.hoover.org/sites/default/files/documents/CLM32MS.pdf).

12. Li Jie, "International System in Transition: From the Perspective of the Financial Crisis," *China International Studies*, May/June 2009, pp. 4–23.

13. Liu Mingfu, *China Dream: Great Power Thinking and Strategic Positioning in the Post-American Age* (Beijing: China Friendship Press, 2009); Guo Yina, "Yan

Xuetong: China Should Provide Neighboring Countries with Military Protection; Eliminate American Power," *International Herald Leader*, Xinhua News Agency, June 1, 2011 (http://news.ifeng.com/mil/4/detail_2011_06/01/6753029_0.shtml).

14. Thom Shanker and Mark Mazzetti, "China and U.S. Clash on Naval Forces," *New York Times*, March 10, 2009 (www.nytimes.com/2009/03/11/world/asia/11military.html).

Notes to Chapter Eight

1. Joint Civilian-Military Investigation Group, "Investigation Result on the Sinking of ROKS 'Cheonan,'" May 20, 2010 (http://news.bbc.co.uk/nol/shared/bsp/hi/pdfs/20_05_10jigreport.pdf); "'North Korean Torpedo' Sank South's Navy Ship," BBC, May 20, 2010 (www.bbc.co.uk/news/10129703).

2. White House, Office of the Press Secretary, "Executive Order Blocking Property of Certain Persons with Respect to North Korea," August 30, 2010 (www. whitehouse.gov/the-press-office/2010/08/30/executive-order-president-blocking-property-certain-persons-with-respect).

3. White House, Office of the Press Secretary, "Remarks by President Obama at G-20 Press Conference in Toronto, Canada," June 27, 2010 (www.whitehouse. gov/the-press-office/remarks-president-obama-g-20-press-conference-toronto-canada).

4. See, for example, the *New York Times* editorial of July 10, 2010, that called the statement "absurdly, dangerously, lame."

5. People's Republic of China, Ministry of Foreign Affairs, "Foreign Ministry Spokesperson Qin Gang's Regular Press Conference on July 15, 2010," July 16, 2010 (www.fmprc.gov.cn/eng/xwfw/s2510/2511/t717494.htm); Yang Yi, "Navigating Stormy Waters: The Sino-American Security Dilemma at Sea," *China Security* 18 (February 2011) (www.chinasecurity.us/images/stories/YangYi.pdf).

6. Siegfried S. Hecker, "What I Found in North Korea," *Foreign Affairs*, December 9, 2010 (http://iis-db.stanford.edu/pubs/23120/What_I_Found_in_North_Korea.pdf).

7. Mark Landler, "Obama Urges China to Check North Koreans," *New York Times*, December 6, 2010 (www.nytimes.com/2010/12/07/world/asia/07diplo.html).

8. Howard Schneider and Scott Wilson, "U.S., South Korea Fail to Reach Free-Trade Deal," *Washington Post*, November 11, 2010 (www.washington post. com/wp-dyn/content/article/2010/11/10/AR2010111006338.html); Martin Fackler, "Obama Speech Marks Shift on North Korea," *New York Times*, November 11, 2010 (www.nytimes.com/2010/11/12/world/asia/12korea.html.

9. Conversations with senior Chinese officials in November 2010.

10. Steve Holland, "No Point Resuming 6-Party North Korea Talks Yet: U.S," Reuters, December 22, 2010 (www.reuters.com/article/2010/12/22/us-korea-

north-obama-idUSTRE6BK4DQ20101222); Chico Harlan, "South Korea's Lee Calls for Six-Party Talks," *Washington Post*, December 29, 2010 (www.washington post.com/wp-dyn/content/article/2010/12/29/AR2010122900863.html), and "'Useful' U.S., China Meetings on North Korea," *Washington Post*, January 6, 2011 (www.washingtonpost.com/wp-dyn/content/article/2011/01/06/AR20110106 02144.html).

11. "Korea's Spy Chief Made Secret Trip to U.S.: Source," Yonhap News Agency, February 17, 2011 (http://english.yonhapnews.co.kr/national/2011/02/17/69/0301000000AEN20110217001300315F.HTML).

Notes to Chapter Nine

1. The release of Aung San Suu Kyi in fact subsequently led to the first signs of an internal thaw in Burma since 1990 and laid the basis for Secretary Clinton to visit in December, 2011.

2. "Obama Urges Burma to Free Suu Kyi," BBC, November 15, 2009 (http://news.bbc.co.uk/2/hi/8361081.stm); "Obama, Asian Leaders Discuss South China Sea," Reuters, September 24, 2010 (www.reuters.com/article/2010/09/24/us-obama-asean-china-seas-idUSTRE68N58O20100924).

3. "Japan Delays Decision on Joining Talks on Pacific Free Trade Accord," Kyodo News Agency, May 17, 2011 (accessed on August 5, 2011, via BBC World-wide Monitoring on Nexis); "Trans-Pacific FTA Negotiating Countries Want Japan in by Nov 2011," Kyodo News Agency, November 24, 2010 (accessed August 5, 2011, via BBC Worldwide Monitoring on Nexis).

4. John Pomfret, "U.S. Floats Plan to Lift Ban on Training Indonesia's Kopas-sus Unit," *Washington Post*, March 3, 2010 (www.washingtonpost.com/wp-dyn/content/article/2010/03/02/AR2010030204053.html).

Notes to Chapter Ten

1. "Remarks at Press Availability—Secretary Hillary Rodham Clinton," Hanoi, Vietnam, July 23, 2010 (www.state.gov/secretary/rm/2010/07/145095.htm).

2. Recounting of Secretary Clinton's and Foreign Minister Yang's remarks based on author's recollections at closed-door meeting of ARF.

3. Mark Landler, "Offering to Aid Talks, U.S. Challenges China on Disputed Islands," *New York Times*, July 23, 2010 (www.nytimes.com/2010/07/24/world/asia/24diplo.html); Edward Wong, "Chinese Military Seeks to Extend Its Naval Power," *New York Times*, April 23, 2010 (www.nytimes.com/2010/04/24/world/asia/24navy.html).

4. Richard Bush, *The Perils of Proximity: China-Japan Security Relations* (Brook-ings, 2010).

5. Keith Bradsher, "Amid Tension, China Blocks Vital Exports to Japan," *New York Times*, September 22, 2010 (www.nytimes.com/2010/09/23/business/ global/ 23rare.html).

6. White House, Office of the Press Secretary, "Press Briefing by Press Secretary Robert Gibbs, Special Assistant to the President and Senior Director for Asian Affairs Jeff Bader, and Deputy National Security Advisor for Strategic Communications Ben Rhodes," September 23, 2010 (http://m.whitehouse.gov/the-press-office/ 2010/09/23/press-briefing-press-secretary-robert-gibbs-special-assistant-president-); U.S. Department of Defense, Office of the Assistant Secretary of Defense (Public Affairs), "DOD News Briefing with Secretary Gates and Admiral Mullen from the Pentagon," September 23, 2010 (www.defense.gov/transcripts/transcript.aspx? transcriptid=4690); Lachlan Carmichael, "Clinton Urges Dialogue to Resolve China-Japan Row," Agence France-Presse, September 23, 2010 (www.google.com/hosted news/afp/article/ALeqM5ir_4TwRS2t5rbIc8_xcgYjzxvoCw).

Notes to Chapter Eleven

1. Barry Eichengreen and Hui Tong, "The External Impact of China's Exchange Rate Policy: Evidence from Firm Level Data," International Monetary Fund Working Paper, July 2011 (www.imf.org/external/pubs/ft/wp/2011/wp11155.pdf); Eswar Prasad, "The U.S.-China Strategic and Economic Dialogue: A Preview of Key Economic Issues," *Brookings Institution Blog*, May 6, 2011 (www.brookings. edu/opinions/2011/0506_us_china_economic_issues_prasad.aspx); William R. Cline and John Williamson, "Currency Wars?" Peterson Institute for International Economics Policy Brief, November 2010 (www.piie. com/ publications/pb/pb10-26.pdf).

2. White House, Office of the Press Secretary, "Statement by the President on the Awarding of the Nobel Peace Prize to Liu Xiaobo," October 8, 2010 (www. whitehouse.gov/the-press-office/2010/10/08/statement-president-awarding-nobel-peace-prize-liu-xiaobo).

3. Conversations with Chinese scholars and think tank analysts in the second half of 2010.

4. Dai Bingguo, "Stick to the Path of Peaceful Development" [in Chinese], *People's Daily*, December 13, 2010 (http://opinion.people.com.cn/GB/13461342.html).

5. U.S. Department of the Treasury, "Secretary Geithner's Remarks on 'The Path Ahead for the U.S.-China Economic Relationship,'" January 12, 2011 (www. treasury.gov/press-center/press-releases/Pages/tg1019.aspx).

6. John Pomfret, "China Tests Stealth Aircraft before Gates, Hu Meet," *Washington Post*, January 11, 2011 (www.washingtonpost.com/wp-dyn/content/article/ 2011/01/11/AR2011011101338.html). For a short analysis of Dai's article, see also Henry Kissinger, *On China* (New York: Penguin Press, 2011), pp. 508–13.

7. White House, Office of the Press Secretary, "U.S.-China Joint Statement," January 19, 2011 (www.whitehouse.gov/the-press-office/2011/01/19/us-china-joint-statement). The language on uranium enrichment was as follows: "The United States and China expressed concern regarding the DPRK's claimed uranium enrichment program. Both sides oppose all activities inconsistent with the 2005 Joint Statement and relevant international obligations and commitments."

8. James Fallows's blog entries can be found on *The Atlantic* website (www.theatlantic.com/james-fallows/page/25/). John Pomfret, "Summit Yields Gains for Both China and U.S.," *Washington Post*, January 21, 2011 (www.washingtonpost.com/wp-dyn/content/article/2011/01/20/AR2011012006311.html); Mark Landler, "U.S. Warning to China Sends Ripples to the Koreas," *New York Times*, January 20, 2011 (www.nytimes.com/2011/01/21/world/asia/21diplo.html?pagewanted=all).

9. Hillary Rodham Clinton, "Inaugural Richard C. Holbrooke Lecture on a Broad Vision of U.S.-China Relations in the 21st Century," U.S. Department of State, January 14, 2011 (www.state.gov/secretary/rm/2011/01/154653.htm).

10. Scott Wilson, "Obama Discusses China's Civil Liberties with Advocates in White House Meeting," *Washington Post*, January 13, 2011 (www.washingtonpost.com/wp-dyn/content/article/2011/01/13/AR2011011306922.html).

Notes to Chapter Twelve

1. Ed O'Keefe, "How the U.S. Government Is Helping Japan," *Washington Post*, March 17, 2011 (www.washingtonpost.com/wp-dyn/content/article/2011/03/17/AR2011031701067.html); Chester Dawson, "U.S. Military Joins in Quake-Relief Effort," *Wall Street Journal*, March 14, 2011 (http://online.wsj.com/article/SB10001424052748704893604576200183092822382.html).

2. Embassy of the United States (Tokyo, Japan), "Travel Warning," March 16, 2011 (http://japan.usembassy.gov/e/acs/tacs-travel20110317.html); Cheryl Pellerin, "Gates Authorizes Humanitarian Funds for Japan, Voluntary Evacuation of Honshu Families," American Forces Press Service, March 17, 2011 (www.army.mil/article/53444/).

3. Embassy of the United States (Tokyo, Japan), "Travel Warning—Japan" (Updated March 21) (http://japan.usembassy.gov/e/acs/tacs-20110321-travel-warning.html); Larry Abramson, "U.S. Makes Iodine Pills Available in Japan, but Cautions against Use," National Public Radio, March 21, 2011 (www.npr.org/blogs/health/2011/03/21/134740081/u-s-makes-iodine-pills-available-in-japan-but-cautions-against-use).

4. Gidget Fuentes, "PACOM Could Evacuate 87,000 Americans," *Army Times*, March 17, 2011 (www.armytimes.com/news/2011/03/navy-pacific-command-prepared-to-evacuate-87k-from-japan-031711/).

5. Gidget Fuentes and Sam Fellman, "Roughead Downplays Odds of Forced Evacuations," *Navy Times*, March 23, 2011 (www.navytimes.com/news/2011/03/navy-roughead-downplays-odds-of-forced-evacuations-032211w/).

NOTES TO CHAPTER THIRTEEN

1. White House, "National Security Strategy," May 2010 (www.whitehouse.gov/sites/default/files/rss_viewer/national_security_strategy.pdf).

2. See Pew Global Attitudes Project, Opinion of the United States, 2007–11 (http://pewglobal.org/database/?indicator=1&survey=13&response=Favorable&mode=map). U.S. favorability ratings since President Obama took office have been up by an average of 12 percent in South Korea, 40 percent in Japan, 58 percent in Indonesia, and 21 percent in China. Frank Ching, "America's Star Is Rising in World Opinion," *Japan Times*, April 30, 2010 (http://search.japantimes.co.jp/cgi-bin/eo20100430fc.html); "S. Koreans Believe Alliance with U.S. Has Grown Stronger," *Chosun Ilbo*, February 9, 2010 (http://english.chosun.com/site/data/html_dir/2010/02/09/2010020900283.html); Retno L. P. Marsudi, "Indonesia, the U.S.: A New Partnership," *Jakarta Post*, April 27, 2009 (www.thejakartapost.com/news/2009/04/27/indonesia-us-a-new-partnership.html); Kang In-sun, "Changing Winds in the S. Korea-U.S. Alliance," *Chosun Ilbo*, July 21, 2010 (http://english.chosun.com/site/data/html_dir/2010/07/21/2010072101145.html); "Japan, U.S. Take Step toward Boosting Alliance," *Yomiuri Shimbun*, April 11, 2011 (www.yomiuri.co.jp/dy/editorial/T110410003473.htm).

Index